Pastina –

My Father's Misfortune, My Mother's Good Soup

by

Joe Ortiz

*The (Mostly) True Stories & Recipes Behind
the Musical "Over The Roof"*

For permission requests, write to the author/publisher at: joe@gocapitola.com

Early Lyrics Publishing—ASCAP
504 Bay Avenue
Capitola, CA 95010

Published by Capitola Gayle's, Inc.
Contact Information: Joe Ortiz: joe@gocapitola.com

Library of Congress Cataloging-in-Publication Data:
ISBN: 979-8-9891943-1-5

Pastina—My Father's Misfortune, My Mother's Good Soup
The (Mostly) True Stories & Recipes Behind the Musical *Over the Roof*
Cover Design: Jana Marcus
Printed in the United States of America 2025
First Edition

Episodes from this book have appeared, in slightly different form, in the following publications and venues:

Feature Articles:
The Santa Cruz Sun, various episodes, 1988-1989
Santa Cruz Weekly, "Pastina—Food for the Soul," 1993
Santa Cruz Weekly, "My Life as a Waitress," 1993
Catamaran Literary Reader. "Prologue and Recipes," Summer 2023,
Vol. 10, Issue 3
Catamaran Literary Reader, "The Fence," Winter 2024, Vol. 12, Issue 1
The Capitola Soquel Times, full book excerpts in monthly installments,
2022-2024

Other books:
The Village Baker, 1993, Ten Speed Press, Berkeley
The Village Baker's Wife, co-authored with Gayle Ortiz, 1997,
Ten Speed Press, Berkeley
The Gardener's Table, co-authored with Richard Merrill, 2000,
Ten Speed Press, Berkeley
Shakespeare on Golf, coauthored with John Tullius, 1997,
Hyperion, New York
Diving into Ink, 2023, Early Lyrics Publishing, Capitola, CA

Musical Productions:
Kitchen Kabaret, 2004, Michael's On Main Restaurant, Soquel, CA
Bread!—The Musical, 2001-2017, Kuumbwa Jazz Center,
Shelton Theater, etc.
Smoke Cabaret, 2001-2017, numerous clubs and theaters
Escaping Queens, 2012 and 2013, Cabrillo Stage, Aptos, CA
Circus, 2019, Cabrillo Stage, Aptos, CA

Table of Contents:

The Recipes:

Preface

BEFORE MY TALE STARTS, it seems wise to tell you a few facts that might help you decipher the logic underlying the family chaos. But first you'll need a bit of background to understand how I found it necessary to add certain assumed incidents to have the story make sense, and why I wrote the memoir in the first place: to find out who I am, and why I behave the way I do.

THE STORY BEGINS when I was six years old in Long Island City, Queens, New York, and ends in Southern California when I was about twelve. My sister, Laura, was fourteen at the start and twenty when it ends and she escaped the house, leaving me alone to parse out my parents' painful separation.

Back in "the projects," as we called our Queens neighborhood, I was a sick, pathetic kid, often ruffled by dicey situations or mangled by angry machinery. But to this day, I don't know if the many predicaments I got into were truly accidental or borne out of my unconscious tactic to hide from my Puerto Rican father's chaotic life and my mother's attempt to buffer his antics.

One of my first memories is of being told to "shut up," causing me to crawl into my shell and go silent. Always being interrupted or spoken over, never being allowed to finish a word or a sentence came with the territory in a household where everyone had an opinion, a voice, and the habit of shouting it right in your face. I'm sure it caused me to cope in what therapists might call "stuffing it," creating the potential for a later eruption—the same outbursts my father frequently made and possibly compelled me to mimic.

Since starting this memoir twenty years ago, my self-therapy has spawned many works of self-expression. For a musical I wrote, titled Escaping Queens, which was produced in two seasons at Cabrillo Stage in 2012 and 2013, I wrote a song about teens who didn't want to become their parents—hardscrabble, savvy kids in the 'hood who, despite their determination to avoid repeating the previous generations' mistakes, couldn't possibly realize the damage had already been done. It seems to me that teenagers learn to recognize their parents' marginal adult behavior and blatant flaws very early on and decide to avoid those influences yet lack the capacity to do so. Since the habits may already have taken root deep inside a child's psyche, I ask myself, "Is it at all possible to escape our parents' affects on us?" Can "breaking the cycle" of child abuse ever be achieved? One way might be for children—after becoming adults—to discover how they were influenced, then create coping mechanisms to learn to process it, and finally, to accept it. Perhaps only then can abused children choose consciously not to be manipulated by past experiences.

In 2024 I took some of the material even further in a short story titled "The Fence," which was published in *The Catamaran Literary Reader*. The story started with actual events but I added so many more fictional scenes that I was compelled to call it fiction. Even though there were fewer made-up events in the musical than in the Fence story—and many less in this memoir you hold in your hand—I learned from that process that many of the invented passages, after being written, rehearsed, and seen performed, virtually became true in my mind. It dawned on me that perhaps kids use imagination as psychological armor. This brought up the idea to me that I must more honestly deal with my family's "escape" from Freddie in the Over the Roof episode in Chapter Thirteen. I state clearly now that that chapter was extensively fabricated.

Finally, in the last few years of revising this memoir, I began to be plagued by the reactionary way I tended to respond to people's criticisms, ribbing, or joking. Through a bit of therapy I started to understand that I was impulsively mimicking my father's bad habits. Could I learn to take a different path? Or would this curse follow me forever?

I started asking myself why I was compelled to follow and even idolize an abusive father. The question popped up in the musical, recast as the question of why my mother put up with my father's abuses. Why did she stay with him? Is there something in her nature and mine that made us willfully submit to and worship an overbearing spouse or parent? Or do we tolerate or even crave the abuse because of our need for some other, self-satisfying reward: the ice cream cone promised, the warmth and safety of a roof over our heads, the security from other, outside storms? Do we react impulsively to suppressed memories, sparked by present-day awkward encounters as our compulsion to repeat new manifestations of the traumas we once experienced?

I do know this: by broaching the difficult topics and admitting I still have the fear of delving deeply into them in my writing, I, at the very least, begin to scratch at the surface of the scab that hides the original pain or trauma. These "baby steps," as a therapist might call them, allow me to start a process of understanding—of going deeper—whether it be in therapy or in story.

I hope to throw some light on these questions in the story to come.

Prologue — A Soup of Bitter Greens

SURE, I KNOW WHAT THEY SAY about too many cooks spoiling the broth—but in our house, back in Long Island City, circa 1952, everybody wanted to stir the soup.

There has never been any question about Italian mothers wearing the apron in their families. My mother, Antonietta Gagliotti Ortiz—an Italian-American housewife married to a Puerto Rican shoemaker—was no exception. Mom ruled the kitchen with a firm but loving hand, and she knew how to put dinner on the table. And it was good.

So, why was everyone else on the block always sticking their heads in Mom's kitchen and stirring up her sauce? Why did husbands, cousins, uncles, and even—on occasion—the family bookie feel the need to say so much as one word about Mom's good soup? A neighborly bit of advice was one thing—there's nothing wrong with someone innocently suggesting a better way to fry a veal cutlet. But wasn't that person, who will remain nameless for the moment, going a bit too far with a quick grind of the pepper mill when Mom wasn't looking?

I guess in a hot-blooded household like ours—where phrases like "Listen to me, Mister," and "Don't get me started" were the very marrow of intimate conversation—food wasn't just something you ate. It was something you talked about. Discussed. Or should I say fought over again and again?

Soup, for example. What is it about soup that arouses our deepest emotions, stirs the blood? And, in the end, how did it save my life?

As a kid I found the soup kettle a comforting sight: the onion, celery, carrot, zucchini, all swirling about in a heady broth, with color, motion, and aroma dancing in the same pot. Safe, soothing, even predictable on occasion. Yet what about the times someone would waltz into Mom's kitchen with a well-meaning secret for giving a little nudge to the flavor? Those so-called surefire remedies could easily unsettle the balance, distracting Mom from the original recipe she'd learned from her own mother. Those remedies—though well-meaning—could easily cause the pot to boil over.

But then there were the good days, when anyone and everyone who passed through our lives had their own unique hand in adding flavor to the finished broth. And to our story.

My sister, Laura—perhaps Mom's biggest pest—always had her hand and nose in one of Mom's dishes. Twelve years old (as the story opens) and streetwise, Laura stole meatballs from the pan, ate raw ravioli dough, and served as the self-appointed guardian angel of the spaghetti sauce. Yes, Mom permitted her to regulate the flavor of her gravy, but nobody else had better lift a spoon to even taste it. Along with Dad, Laura always had a special affinity for the pepper mill. As Mom's chief helper and nemesis, she had an opinion about everything, from soup to nuts, and she was always ready to get right in your face and tell you all about it. That is, until the back of Dad's hand got in the way.

And Dad? He stirred the pot, all right. He hollered at Mom when dinner was late, roared like an animal when he smelled something burning (but refused to get up from his cozy spot on the couch), never failed to mention when the meatloaf needed more salt, and complained to high heaven when the aglio e olio (that's pasta with garlic and oil) wasn't spicy enough for a Puerto Rican's taste buds. "More pepper flakes, Nonny. More pepper flakes!" he would thunder. One night he recited his entire recipe for arroz con pollo while lounging on the couch smoking Camels and picking lint from between his toes. Poor Mom had to crane her neck out the kitchen doorway and listen to him squawk—all the while taking notes with one hand and making her famous meatballs with the other. (Have you ever tried to roll a meatball with one hand? Mom sure could!)

Many an afternoon I remember relatives and neighbors sitting around the table puffing cigarettes and sipping little tumblers of red wine, discussing the important things in life: how to reduce a broth without "bruising" it, how to sauté the onions to darken a soup, how to boil a chicken without drying it out. Naturally, these food tales were heavily peppered with the events of the day: the fishing trips to Coney Island gone sour, the pieces of furniture Dad lost in a bet, the promised Dodgers tickets that never materialized. But for the most part, the conversation always came back to food: most specifically either tomato sauce—which we called "gravy"—or soup.

In our house soup came in many forms. Everyone had a favorite. Take vegetable soup, or minestrone, for example. Some said you started it with what we know today as a mirepoix (a mixture of diced celery, onion, and carrot), nurtured gently in olive oil over low heat. Then, you'd add your other vegetables and sauté them for a while, adding stock and allowing it all to meld together with a good dousing of olive oil until the vegetables were to your liking. But Dad had his own no-nonsense approach: "Ahhh, just trow everything into da pot and let it cook, fa chrissake!"

The savory magic of pasta and beans was irresistible. The Sicilians in our neighborhood called it pasta fazool. Every region had their own pronunciation, anything from "fazoo" to "fagiol" and everything in between. (Mimicking them all, my dad called it Pasta fa Joey). If you put ten Sicilians, ten Neapolitans, and ten Venetians in a room, you'd probably be offered a couple of hundred excellent variations of this peasant delicacy.

And Ah! There was pasta lenticchie. Or what my mother called "pasta lendique." A simple blend of boiled lentils and tubetti pasta, this earthy combination could send me swooning with its rich, meaty flavor. Years later, Laura and I would argue for hours about whether Mom started her lentil soup with a ham hock, a slice of bacon, or a few diced aromatic vegetables. "You're supposed to know," I would scream at my sister, with the same venom I'd learned from all the rest of them back then (feeling sheepishly apologetic a moment later).

Then there was pastina—star macaroni in rich broth. Probably my favorite, and what my story is all about. But minestrone was often a close rival, ever the antagonist—an equal but valiant foil.

If pastina represented all the curative blessings of chicken broth, its little pasta "stars" suspended in a translucent liquid firmament, then minestrone was the reality—the colorful chaos of vegetables, like sticks and stones tumbling in an earthy broth. If pastina epitomized my mother's nurturing, minestrone represented Dad's dark and reckless abandon. If pastina brought hope and salvation, minestrone symbolized our shadowy hopes of ever escaping Queens.

As you can guess, I often sided with Mom's favorite: the soul-soothing broth and pasta. My first bowl? Mom sat me on a phone book at the dining room table. After setting the steaming bowl of pastina in front of me, she lifted a spoonful into my mouth. Well, I guess I made a face, because Mom said, "Oh, I forgot to get Parmesan at the grocery! But I'll get some tomorrow. I promise! Now eat!"

What is pastina? My Aunt Mary called it a "belly wash," a phrase that got a laugh every time she said it, even if no one could ever explain what it meant. Mary always said—and most aunts, mothers, godmothers, and grandmothers would agree—that pastina could cure the common cold. Made with a rich, concentrated chicken broth and tiny specks of star pasta and garnished with a little chopped parsley and a sprinkle of grated Parmesan at the table, pastina lifted many of the woes from our lives. It was golden. And glistening. And when steaming hot, the rich saltiness of the broth seemed to cut right through any stress, mild or aggravated.

As long as I was hypnotized by all the aromas and flavors that surrounded me, I felt safe. I lived in a thick ethnic ragout of food, argument, and activity. But pastina, and in fact any peasant soup, was the redemptive salve for any wound.

So, sit down at the table with a little glass of something to drink and watch what happens. As best as I can remember, this is how the story all began . . .

Between the chapters you'll see . . .

. . . THE LITTLE BITS OF GLOSS that have helped me recraft the story after years of fine-tuning the details and revisiting the delights and the agonies—exploring the truths and inventions I made to discover what really happened.

The idea of inserting these mini excursions was inspired by a suggestion from poet Stuart Kestenbaum at a Shakerag (Tennessee) workshop in July 2023. Stuart gave us a writing prompt to jar us out of our safe writing practice and into more daring revelations about scenes, images, or situations. Whatever the prompt was that day, it forced me to put a new perspective on my story.

After I read what I had written to the class, Stuart said it sounded like a dramatic monologue—which I mistakenly heard as "traumatic monologue." I grabbed onto that idea, which led me to uncover important emotional experiences I had previously been afraid to explore.

Not wanting to upset the flow of the existing story arc by interjecting these confessions into the narrative, I decided to use them as connective tissue. I hope they show readers how the revisionist narrative of a man-child 60 years later might rear its head from the hazy amber patina of childhood projection—influenced by my need to hide, distort, and make palatable the painful experiences themselves.

In revisiting these experiences as an adult, I now understand that I was only able to remember what I was prepared to look at truthfully. And because I couldn't recall the specifics of certain events, I may have tended to fabricate narratives in order to make sense out of the chaos of my own childhood abuse. With uncertain yet sincere caution I have penned these monologues in hopes of understanding the doubts and confusions of many years.

La Famiglia - The Family: Joey, Mom, Laura, and Dad

Chapter One:
Playing Dice and Baking Eggplant

MY FATHER FLIPPED THE QUARTER with his thumb; it flew up in an arc and landed flush against the baseboard underneath the red Formica table in our dining room in Queens. He and I were tossing coins for money. To me it was a fun game, but according to Mom—who stood a few steps away in the kitchen making dinner—it was just another bad habit Dad was teaching me.

Everywhere Dad went, a heavy olfactory cloud followed him around like weather: the rank but somehow intoxicating smell of beer and cigarettes mixed with the shoe-leather dust he carried home with him from the shoe-repair shop.

That cloud hung over us now as we flipped coins against the wall. And you can bet that the counterpoint of Mom and Dad's different aromas, let alone their heated opinions about what was good for me, was a balance you didn't dare upset. If I whined, or sided too much with either one, I'd find myself like a little rowboat in a storm, getting battered back and forth. Maybe I'd get scolded. Or slapped. If I complained, I'd only have to wait longer for dinner.

Instinctively, I knew that to enjoy a decent meal, I had to put up with Dad's push and Mom's pull.

Dad was down in the squat made famous by peasants through-

13

out the world, crouching flat-footed, his butt nearly touching the floor, having learned this stance in the jungles outside of San Juan where he'd grown up. He said it came in handy whether you were groveling down below the canopy of trees "doing your business" or squatting under some streetlamp in the Old Ciudad playing dice.

"Do ya get the similarities, Joey?" He whispered so Mom couldn't hear him: "That's why they call it . . ." Dad stopped. He mouthed the word: "craps." He nodded his head and smiled, then hunkered down to see if Mom was listening.

Mom was silent. But the moment we heard her shuffling around, Dad knew he could say anything and get away with it. So we waited.

In the meantime, I had to play Dad's game whether I liked it or not, whether we were flipping quarters, or someday, playing dice like he'd always promised. Dad made all the rules. At least out in the dining room.

The kitchen was another story. That's where Mom had her say. As long as Dad and I could hear her chopping, mixing, frying, we knew we could play our game in peace. The minute she put the knife down and it got quiet in there, though, Dad and I would hold our breath. I'd learned all this from Dad. But he didn't always take his own advice. Like a moment later, when his quarter slid up against the wall and he pointed to it and screamed out like a banshee:

"A winner, Joey! Only a leaner can beat me."

His victory fired up his ego, his anger-driven need for dominance. He placed his wrists below his belt and used his forearms to hoist his pleated blue gabardine pants up like a gangster in a mobster movie. When the pants rose above his black French-toed shoes you could see he didn't have on any socks; he never wore them. Dad's sleeveless undershirt—which I'd heard many neighbors refer to as a "wife-beater"—revealed a tattoo on his shoulder, an ornate scroll that read "Mother." I'm not making this up. The blue ink of the tattoo was the same color as the veins that heaved and throbbed along his muscular arms and face when he got this worked up.

Just then, Laura burst through the front door, her fiery pigtails bouncing around her freckled face, her dungarees rolled up to the calves. She circled around and taunted us, waving her hand over our coins. She threw off her Dodgers cap and leaned her sawed-off broomstick wrapped in black tape in the corner—a clear sign that she hadn't been at Glee Club as Mom believed, but down on the stoop playing stickball with a bunch of guys.

This fourteen-year-old whirlwind kept both Mom and Dad on their toes by constantly stirring the pot. She sang doo-wop down on the corner with the guys, but she could also whip every last one of them at stoopball by knocking a Spaldeen over the

chain link fence of the handball courts behind the Queensborough Projects.

As far as *a cappella* singing was concerned, she could pull off a sweet rendition of Judy Garland's "Somewhere Over the Rainbow." Take your pick—June Christie, Joni James, Julie London, Chris Conner, Rosemary Clooney—Laura could imitate the finer shadings of each and every voice. And you could hear the difference.

Laura ran into the kitchen, kissed Mom on the cheek, and went straight to the Victrola. But instead of spinning a Nat Cole or Judy Garland record, she turned on the radio and started flipping the dial in that aggravating thud-thud sound that drove us all crazy.

"I'm warning you," Dad said. "Shut it off and go wash ya hands fa dinner."

Laura disappeared into the bathroom.

Mom was in the kitchen, preparing another of her specialties, Eggplant Parmesan, and had arrived at the step that caused so much argument in our family: whether to use grated Parmesan cheese in beaten egg to coat the eggplant before you fried it. "That's an old wives' tale," Mom would always say. She had learned her method from her mother, who came from Basilicata, where you were taught to make do with what you had and keep it simple. Some recipes call for layering the eggplant with mozzarella, but in Basilicata they leave it out: Cocina Povera, was what they called it. But it was poor only in ingredients, not in peasant flavor.

According to Mom, it was the way you coated the eggplant slices with salt, drained them in a colander to release the moisture, then fried the slices in a skillet of bubbling olive oil that gave them a crispy crust and a rich, custard-like texture inside.

"Hot oil," Mom said. "Hot, hot olive oil, with well-drained eggplant. That's it! Oh, of course, you flavor the oil by sautéing a little garlic in it." But that hardly had to be said.

When Mom started the frying, a thick, heady aroma of garlic in fruity olive oil floated into the diningroom and the sound gave Dad and me our cover.

"Come on, Joey," Dad finally said. "Pay attention to da game." I felt defeated. I was getting hungrier by the minute. But dinner was a long way off.

"Come on, Joey," he said. "Play."

Just then Laura burst back into the diningroom.

"When's dinner?" Laura said as she walked over to the Victrola and pulled a 78 out of its sleeve.

"Laura," Dad said, not even turning his head to look at her. "Put on 'Fever' one more time and I'm gonna give you a shot in the head." She played her favorite song so often you could almost hear the throbbing bass line before the needle hit vinyl.

But instead we heard the sweet and gentle groove of Julie London singing "Cry Me a River." When Laura started to whine about dinner again, Dad said, "Shut up," only louder this time. "We'll eat when we eat. Ya mutha's cookin' her heart out. Joey and I are pitchin' quarters."

So, Laura turned on her heels and headed for the door.

"Where ya goin'," Dad said. "Dinner's gonna be ready in a . . ."

But it was too late. Laura had already slammed the door behind her; instantly, another record clicked down the spindle and onto the turntable and the sultry voice of Peggy Lee filled the apartment:

Never knew how much I loved you. Never knew how much I cared.

"I'm gonna kill her," Dad said, sounding like a ferocious jungle cat ready to pounce. In our house you could get smacked for much less than playing 'Fever' for only about the thousandth time.

The chaos drove me crazy. I had to check out for a while, escaping into the patterns and textures of our living room, the same splash and color that Mom used in her cooking. A pillow of every shape and size, covered in teal and burgundy fabric with a fuzzy fringe around the edges. Drapes of a floral design. A rug of dots and paisley.

Protected by all the textures surrounding me, I was also hypnotized by the sizzle of eggplant frying, the sweet smell of garlic.

Dad poked me again and went on talking. He had told me about leaners before: they were "as rare as a whitie in Harlem," he said. Except the night Eddie Ryan threw the leaner of his life, beating Dad out of sixteen dollars and change, a whole day's wages for a shoemaker in Queens in 1952.

Dad swore that Eddie had put some sealing wax on his quarter to make it stick, but he couldn't prove it. "Ya not supposed ta touch another guy's coin," Dad had explained. He told me all about what he called Eddie's "rotten luck," and about how much money Dad had lost, but I wasn't supposed to tell Mom. "She finds out and things'll get a whole lot stranger than normal around here," he said. Why was he turning careful on me? I thought he got a kick out of stirring Mom up.

Fortunately for Dad she was inside stirring up the gravy. So, Dad went on.

"Snap out of it, Joey," Dad said, but I couldn't budge. Finally, he tugged my arm and taunted me with his sing-song routine: "Na, na, na, NaNa. You gotta get a leaner to beat me."

I tried to deflect.

"But what about the tomato sauce, Mom?" I yelled in to her.

"Soon, Joey, Soon," Ma said. But it didn't work to settle Dad.

"Come on, Joey. It's your turn. The game, fa cryin' out loud. Ya gotta get a leaner to BEAT ME."

"BEAT YOU," I thought. It triggered an old memory and the terror those words called up. Instinctively, I raised my arm at Dad. And he exploded.

"Don't raise ya hand to me, Mister," Dad said, putting his own hand on his belt. And the word "mister"—clothed in the steely knife-like edge of his voice—would it be enough to make him erupt like he did? Like a volcano?

"No, Daddy, No," I said, trembling. I went back quickly into my trance. Suddenly, a raging white fire blazed in front of my eyes. I wanted to run to Mom. But instead, I froze.

Just then, my mother's voice echoed out of the kitchen, like an angel: "I'm making the tomato sauce, Joey," she said. "Come on in and watch. It's easy."

Was it Mom's angelic voice that saved me? Or was it the sauce?

DAD JUST SAT THERE, staring at the wall, scraping together what few coins he had left. As I sat there trembling, Dad settled back into his squat on the floor, silently grabbing a few of the coins I had won from him and tossing them back into his own pile.

But Dad and I still had some of our coins scattered on the floor in front of us, so I guessed the game was still on.

"No, Mom, you can do the sauce," I yelled. "We're still playing."

Dad motioned to me to make my throw. I could feel my chest raging. Without thought, I made a defiant, over-handed wind-up and flung the quarter against the wall. When my quarter knocked Dad's coin away and bounced inside of his, he started to fume again.

"Ya beat me, Joey. Again!" Dad screamed. "Ya took all my money."

"H-E-R-M-A-N!" my mother's voiced boomed out of the kitchen, and she glared at us from the doorway. In one hand she held a plate of flour, and in the other a slice of eggplant ready to be dredged and fried. She dropped the slice in the flour, gave it a snap to dust off the excess, then shook her finger at Dad.

"Leave him alone," she said. "He's just a kid."

"Nonny," Dad said. "This Palooka's takin' all my change."

"Herman, what kinda stuff is this ta be teachin' a six-year-old?"

When Mom turned back toward the stove, Dad hunkered down toward me and whispered, "Don't pay any attention to ya mutha, Joey. She doesn't know about games. She thinks we're gamblin'. But we're just playin', huh, Joey?"

Then he said loudly toward the kitchen, "Leaners pay double, Joey."

You could hear Mom growling above the sound of the bubbling olive oil. We heard a big splat and a loud sizzle as Mom dropped each slice into the skillet. I was so hungry I began to fantasize about dancing slices of eggplant. Would we ever eat?

"Ya gotta let me get revenge, Joey," Dad said.

Dad started tugging at me again, and dragged me into the living room, away from Mom.

When Mom wasn't around, Dad always brought out the dice. He showed me how they rolled even though they were square, how the numbers always bounced up in different combinations and how—just when you figured out their pattern of turning up the numbers you wanted—that pattern would change.

Dad walked toward me, carrying the dice between his thumb and forefinger, gazing at them as if they were diamonds. Dad smooshed up his face like a clown and pumped his eyebrows as if to say "I'm a hot shot."

"Remremba' when I told ya not to touch these," Dad said, fingering the dice. "Mommy might get mad," he whined.

"But you're learning to play, mister. So, I can win back my money."

"Herman," Mom yelled, louder this time. She walked out into the living room. With auburn hair and a creamy white complexion, she didn't look anything like someone whose parents were from southern Italy. The rest was typical: she wore a bandanna around her head, stockings knotted down below the knees, and fluffy blue slippers. Waving a wooden spoon coated with what most anyone else in the world would call tomato sauce but what everyone in Queens called gravy, she said:

"I don't want Joey learnin' about dice."

Then Mom just let out a big gasp of frustration and went back to the stove.

"These are da magic bones, Joey," Dad said. "Seven's the numba you want ta come up. So, you call for a seven." What did he mean?

"Hold up ya dukes," Dad said. I backed off. I held up my clenched fists anyway. When Dad reached toward me, I flinched. But then he gently spread my fingers, pointed to one hand, and said, "How much is dat?"

"Five," I said. Then he grabbed two fingers of my other hand and said, "Five and two is seven. That's ya lucky numba. Now say, 'Come on, seven'."

"Come on, seven," I said.

"Six and one is seven. Four and three is seven. Five and two is seven," he said. "Lotsa combinations. Lotsa chances fa ya numba ta come up. You just have ta believe in your numba. You gotta have faith."

"FAITH, Herman?" Mom's voice resounded out of the kitchen, echoing off the plaster walls. "Faith has nothing to do with dice, Herman. It has to do with believing in Jesus, not in silly numbers. And luck."

But Daddy went on as if Mom had said nothing.

"Ya have to be careful of snake eyes, Joey," he whispered. "That's one and one and it's called craps."

"Herman!"

Mom came out yelling this time. She was shaking the spoon, splattering gravy everywhere. "I hate that word and I hate that game. And I don't want you teaching Joseph how to gamble. Now put those dice away."

"Nonnie," he said. "Just let me see if I can win my money back from this smart-aleck kid. I guarantee ya I can beat him in ten minutes. He doesn't know the odds."

"You don't either, Herman. You're aggravating me."

He shook his head and sighed a big breath.

"Dat's it, Joey," Dad said. "Ya got all my money. Mommy says we can't play no more. It's all her fault."

What could I say? Dad curled up on the couch and hid behind his newspaper.

"You promised about the dice, Dad." I said to him, sheepishly.

Dad just stared at me: "Never mind," he said. "You think about it too much and you make yourself sick." When Dad finally put the dice back into his pocket, I knew the game was over. Then we heard Mom slide the casserole onto the oven rack.

"Sometimes you get on a bad roll," he said. "You roll the dice and roll them some more, and your number never comes up. That's when you gotta do something to change your luck."

So I took his advice and went into the kitchen, where I jumped up on a stool near the stove.

Mom picked up a pan containing the rest of the sauce. She cooled it with her breath and spooned some into my mouth. I could hear the eggplant begin to sizzle in the oven—that enticing sound of cheese starting to bubble and brown with a rich, milky coating that would make the top dark and crusty.

I was disappointed at not being able to even touch the dice, let alone play. But I was so hungry, my stomach started churning like the Big Dipper at Coney Island. Only a taste of Mom's good Eggplant Parmesan could cure all that.

Strongly Remembered Experiences, Real:

I CONVINCED MYSELF long ago that my most strongly remembered experiences were real. They were etched on my brain through many years of reflection. But events that were only partially remembered still remain hazy; like dreams, they go largely ignored or are only given a glance on occasion, stored on a back shelf in the attic of my mind.

Early on in the writing process, I was able to distinguish events I remembered accurately from those I may have heard whispered about in the stairwell or at the kitchen table as a child. Only later, the repressed or fragmented memories were reinforced by momentary insights that flashed into my mind, seemingly for no reason. Those once-muddy images attained a new shade of mystery and started to make sense, giving me a path forward in my understanding and acceptance.

These new flashes of insight of how certain incidents were connected served to reinforce what was once a phantom belief, a puzzling curiosity: "Why would Dad give the apartment over to the bookie? Was it to settle a bad gambling debt?" Other similar questions rattled around in my brain. But nothing got answered definitively.

Finally—through my dwelling on certain events, writing them down, years of therapy—those once-hazy questions that hid in a deep recess of my memory became clearer. But now there's still a resistance. I refuse to look at the gory details.

I'm guessing that a willingness to look deeper often only arrives incrementally—if at all. But will I ever be willing to go into "the dark room"—my terrifying cavern of self-discovery?

Maybe not yet. Maybe tomorrow. Maybe never.

Chapter Two:
Aspirin for Dinner?
Or, Finally the Eggplant?

JUST AS DAD BEGAN SLIPPING into his shoes after frantically searching around the house for a fresh pack of smokes, Mom leaned her head out of the kitchen doorway and said:

"Don't run out to the store tonight, Herman. Please?"

You could hear the oven door squeak as Mom pulled the bubbling casserole out of the oven and placed it on a cooling rack. "This eggplant Parmesan's gotta cool for twenty minutes," she said.

Dad was already halfway out the door.

"Herman, I mean it," Mom said. "Don't go! Ya got a bottle of Rheingold in the fridge and a half pack of Camels on the Victrola."

Dad grumbled something under his breath, then reluctantly settled back into his chair and hid behind the newspaper.

"When Laura gets back from wherever she ran off to this time," Mom said, "have her set the table, wouldja?" She untied her apron and threw it on the drainboard.

"Herman?" But the paper only rustled.

"I'm going down ta Angie's," Mom said, harping to the back of the sports page. "I've got to get a little parsley fa the top of the eggplant. Stay here, will ya?"

Eggplant slices after frying.

Dad dropped the paper to his lap and glared at her.

"Herman, did ya hear me?"

"Sure, sure, sure," Dad said. "Go already, go."

Mom blew a big, exaggerated breath into the air, and ran out. The moment the door slammed, Dad jumped up and threw the paper on the couch.

"Joey, I'll be right back," he said. "Stay away from the stove or Mommy'll get mad. Laura will be home any minute."

As soon as I was alone, I was free. Free from my parents arguing about gambling. About doctor bills. About Dad's drinking. About me getting sick all the time. Having been a sponge to absorb it all, I'd learned from them the patter of their constant bickering. Words like "headache," "bellyache," "pain," "fever," rattled in my brain. I strung my parents' litany of phrases together as my own fantasy story:

"Freddie is a real headache," I mimicked my mother's voice out loud, talking about the neighborhood bookie who always hounded Dad for money. "Quitcha bellyachin', Nonnie," I said to myself, just as Dad might have answered. I went on in alternating voices: *I only lost three dollars . . . It's fa Joey's doctor bill . . . I got a big deal goin' in the mornin'. . . This is aggravating, HERMAN! . . .*

Just then Laura ran in. "Joey, ya talking to yourself again?" she said. "I saw Dad downstairs. He said to keep an eye on ya. Whataya gonna do, Joey, turn into a pumpkin?"

"Laura, DON'T!" I said. "I'm just playing."

"Ya not gonna get sick on me, are ya? Mom would slap me real good if ya did." Before I could answer, she went into the living room and got so involved in a magazine that I became invisible.

When Laura said, ya not gonna get sick, I thought about Dr. Boccardi and what he prescribed after every visit. So, I mimicked Boccardi too: Just give him an aspirin, Annie, and put him to bed. Aspirin was one of my favorite foods. Not baby aspirin, but the real thing; I enjoyed its tangy taste. I started to dwell on the aspirin in the kitchen cabinet. Lost in her magazine, Laura was oblivious, so I went into the kitchen, climbed up on a chair, and grabbed the aspirin bottle. I unscrewed the cap and took out a single pill. Then I jumped down, ran past Laura, and went into the bedroom. I lay down on Mom and Dad's bed and chewed the aspirin until it was gone.

"You're a real pill," I said to myself, out loud again. "Quitcha bellyaching," I answered.

Mom and Dad hadn't come back, so I tried to stretch my luck. I went into the kitchen, got one more aspirin from the bottle, ran back into the bedroom, and again lay down to finish it off. I continued, one aspirin at a time, until I'd eaten more than I could count. I kept wondering if I'd get caught. I enjoyed the tension of not knowing. I was beginning to feel my stomach churning, but I didn't know if it was from guilt or from medicine.

As I slipped into the kitchen for the half-dozenth time, Mom walked in the door. She saw that Dad wasn't there and blew her stack. "Daddy left you alone again," she mumbled through her teeth. She looked at my face and could see something was wrong.

"Joey, ya look green," she said. "What'sa matta?"

She glanced into the kitchen and saw the chair by the counter and the cabinet door open and started to panic. She put me to bed immediately and stuck a thermometer in my mouth. Then she ran to the phone to call Dr. Boccardi.

In the bedroom, I started convulsing with hot flashes, my mouth wide open but no air coming in. Mom, seeing me gasping for breath and feeling helpless, screamed at the top of her lungs for Dad, who happened to be walking in the door with his beer and smokes. He ran into the bedroom, took me in his arms, and breathed air into my mouth as if his own life depended on it. At that point the fever seemed to break, and he laid me back onto the bed where, they tell me, I fell into a calm, peaceful sleep.

When Dr. Boccardi arrived, I woke up and found myself wrapped in a blanket on the couch. He took my temperature.

"One-O-Four," he said as Mama howled.

"He's going to be okay," Dr. Boccardi said, his brown suit warm and rich as hot chocolate, his tender eyes always sympathetic enough to soothe me—reminding me I was going to be all right.

"Joseph," Dr. Boccardi finally said. "How many aspirin did you eat?"

I hesitated at first. Since I could hardly think and barely speak, I fumbled with my fingers, trying to calculate the number. I stuck up one, then two, then three . . .

As Mom grew impatient, she prodded me: "How many?" she said. "Come on!"

Just then Laura walked in and echoed the same question: "How many, Joey? Come on."

"Come on," I said in a daze.

Impulsively, I held up five fingers on my left hand and two on my right.

"Come on . . . seven."

MY MOTHER HOWLED the moment she realized I wasn't calling for the dice to "roll my number" as Dad had taught me but confessing to have eaten seven aspirin. Doctor Boccardi quickly calmed her down.

"It'll be okay, Annie," Boccardi said, as if he'd seen the situation a million times.

"Give him a plate of aglio e olio—without too much garlic—put him to bed and he'll be fine."

For once the prescription was not for aspirin.

"What about the Eggplant Parmesan?" Dad chimed in, poking his head into the bedroom.

"Now, Herman," Boccardi said. "You know Eggplant Parmesan's

~ *Ortiz*

even better the next day. Besides, Joseph needs something gentle. The garlic will cut the acidity of the aspirin and the pasta will soothe the aggravation to his stomach. Tomorrow, a little white rice throughout the day, and maybe some pastina for dinner and by the weekend he'll be eating gravy again."

"Maybe even a taste of eggplant," Mom said.

"If there's any left," Dad said, winking at me. But I was in no mood to be kidded.

Mom glared at Dad the whole time Boccardi lectured them. Mom finally realized that, in all the commotion, she hadn't had the chance to give Dad hell for leaving me alone. When Dad saw Mom stewing, he tried to divert her anger by appearing concerned. After he found out it was aspirin, he said:

"He's gonna have agita tonight. Just give him some Briochkey."

Briochkey was the medicinal cure for any form of indigestion. A foul, milky liquid, it was designed to coat your stomach. Used often and always on hand, Briochkey promised the same cure as Amaro, the dark Italian liqueur used as a *degustivo,* or digestive remedy, except the women favored Briochkey, whereas the men leaned toward treating overeating and drinking with another shot of booze.

"Briochkey's not a good idea, Herman," Boccardi said.

"Sure, Herman," Mom said, still fuming. "You'd fight medicine with medicine." End of discussion.

Mom said the aglio e olio would be perfect. "We can eat it for dinner too. And save the eggplant fa tomorrow."

Dad screwed up his face as if Puerto Ricans didn't like pasta with garlic and olive oil the way Italians do.

When he told Mom he was going to walk Dr. Boccardi down to the bus stop, she gave Dad a look that said she knew he was leaving to escape her wrath.

Mom just nodded her head toward me and stared at Dad.

Mom at Aunt Rose's wedding

So, he picked me up, blanket and all, and carried me from the bedroom to the dinner table and sat me on a chair.

When a knock came at the door, Dad opened it to find our downstairs neighbor, Mrs. Vynella, standing right there in the hall. As Dad and Dr. Boccardi went out, Mrs. Vynella came in.

"*Aglio e olio*, right Annie?" Mrs. Vynella said. She claimed she knew as much as Dr. Boccardi. She knew I'd taken aspirin before anyone had told her, because I'd done it before. She always tried to convince Mom we could avoid all the doctor bills if we'd just listen to her instead. "And what if it's something serious?" Mom would say to her.

"Whatdawhy know?" Mrs. Vynella said. "All kids fall, scuff their knees, and get into medicine."

"Joey's doctor bills are already $56," Mom said. "Last week he had bronchitis. Then a kid at nursery hit him on the head with a sandbox shovel and he needed three stitches.

"And Herman's no help," Mom went on. "He's always got a deal goin'. If the deal works out, we wind up with baseball tickets. Or a piece of furniture. It's how we got the Victrola.

"And if a deal goes bad," Mom said, "We lose money. It's just Herman's excuse to gamble."

"It's not gambling, Ma," I said. "It's playin'."

"Don't stick up fa ya fatha, Joey," Mrs. Vynella said. "He's a real louse."

"ANGIE," Mom said. "Don't talk like that in front of Joseph."

"Well, Annie," Mrs. Vynella said. "You just . . ."

"Nevermind," Mom said. "He's my husband. I can say it. Don't you say it. Especially in front of my son."

"Okay, Annie, Okay."

"Yeah, sure," Mom went on. "Herman's impossible. If it's baseball tickets, he's gone to Brooklyn all day. No work."

"And ya know there's a lot of bars over there, Annie . . . "

"STOP IT, OKAY?!?" Mom just stared at her and cocked her head toward me.

Mrs. Vynella finally clammed up. She started for the door.

"I know what you're goin' through Ann, tisk, tisk. But what can you do?"

It was hard to believe Mrs. Vynella admitting she didn't have an answer. Even so, she'd suggest an ancient remedy. She would offer you something to eat:

"Come down again," she said. "You'll need more parsley for the aglio e olio."

"'S parsley good for eating too much aspirin?"

"I don't know nuthin' from aspirin," said Mrs. Vynella. "But parsley's great for agita. You'd pay Boccardi six dollars to find that out."

WHEN DAD GOT BACK from his walk with the doctor, Mom jumped all over him: "What'd Boccardi say, Herman?"

"He says we should move ta Arizona fa Joey's bronchitis," he said. "But that's crazy."

"I know all about Arizona, Herman. Every time I talk to Boccardi, he tells me the weather there would be healthier for Joseph's lungs. But you know I'm not talking about Arizona, Herman. What'd he say about the doctor bill?"

"Boccardi told me it's all right. We can pay when we got it. He said he'd give us another few weeks."

"Herman," Mom yelled. "You always say that. But Boccardi's just being nice. What if Joey keeps getting sick? If he knows we can't pay, Boccardi might not come for a house call. I don't like this."

"Nonnie, what kinda doctor would neglect a sick kid because his parents got no money to pay the bill? I guarantee ya, he's not that way."

"Your guarantees are like the Bums winning the Pennant, Herman," Ma said. "It never happens."

But Dad had his way of holding out. About money, and about dinner, too. Since Mom knew he hated spaghetti aglio e olio, she cut him a slice of eggplant now that it had finally cooled.

Dad sat at the table across from me and started to eat. Then

Dad went into his little singing-talking routine that made me know he was ribbing me: "Ya coulda had eggplant if you didn't decide ta eat aspirin fa dinner, Joey."

"Herman. Leave him alone."

I was disappointed about missing out on eggplant, even though my stomach told me it was the right thing to do.

Mom said she was going to eat with me. As Dad dug into his melanzane, Mom put on a pot of water to boil and started to peel four cloves of garlic. Just as she began to smash them with the side of the knife, she remembered what the doctor had said. So she put three of the cloves back in the garlic dish and instead minced one clove very fine.

She pulled out the box of spaghetti, slid some out and held a small amount of it in front of my face.

"That much is for two," she said, holding it up tightly between her thumb and index finger to show me how to measure. I was too sick to care. She poured a small handful of salt into the pot of boiling water.

"The magic ingredient for aglio olio is water, Joey," she said. "Like for all good pasta, water helps ta bind the oil and macaroni into a sauce.

"Better ya should learn to cook than learn to gamble. It's a lot safer."

Dad just twisted up his face again, snarled toward the kitchen, and went on eating.

"Just take the chopped garlic," Mom said, "and fry it in a couple of tablespoons of olive oil for a few seconds. But don't burn it or it'll get bitter. When the pasta's very al dente, that's still a little firm to the bite, you put the pasta in the pan with the oil and garlic. Add some of the pasta water and cook it down. Turn it a lot—*gira molto,* my mother used to say. That turns the oil and water into a creamy sauce. When the water cooks off and the pasta's done, add a nice little handful of chopped parsley—turn off the heat and that's it. All it needs is some grated Parmesan at the table."

Although the first bite of the pasta in garlic and oil started to turn my stomach, quickly it began to go down just fine. It made me feel better. The two or three spoonfuls I couldn't finish, Mom ate. Then she made Dad take me to bed.

ON THE WAY INTO THE BEDROOM—Dad again carrying me wrapped in my blanket—I reminded him about sitting with me until I nodded off. I was afraid of the dark, so in order to fall asleep, I needed to hold onto one of my parents' arms. As Dad brought me in, laid me down and covered me, he said, "I'm getting tired of sitting here while ya fall asleep, Joey. Someday I'm going to make a fake arm outta leather for you to hold onto."

"No, Daddy, No."

"I'm only foolin'," he said sarcastically. He thought boys shouldn't cry, and any hint of that from me would drive him raging crazy. But I was too sick to need an arm that night. Too sick to be kidded; too wasted even to cry.

After Dad tucked me in and left, I still needed the cowgirls, though. The fairy cowgirls that guarded my bed were my protective angels. They were modeled after Dale Evans, but they looked more like Rita Hayworth and Lana Turner: robust, healthy women who rode horses through my room at night while my parents and Laura sat up watching TV. I'm sure the sound of the music echoing through the hall was the catalyst for my fantasizing.

The cowgirls twirled their lassos, roped me and tied me up. They sang cowboy songs and built campfires and I could almost smell the aroma of smoke floating through the bedroom. Because these beautiful women were around, I felt safe until I fell asleep. They softened my bruises and calmed my stomach.

And, sure, I guess they even sheltered me from the brutal

35

sounds of Mom and Dad when they came to bed and struggled around with one another while they thought I was fast asleep.

The cowgirls wore chaps and holsters and guns. Their hats bobbed up and down around their necks as they rode their stallions across the bedroom walls. The cowgirls, with their long, flowing hair and romantic eyes, were more real to me that Amos 'n' Andy, the Honeymooners, and the Brooklyn Dodgers. They were as delicious as pizza and Chinese food, as soothing as spaghetti aglio e olio and pastina. They were as important as Superman, Hopalong Cassidy, Jacky Robinson, and the Cisco Kid.

Later that night Dad came in and said, "Who you talking to, Joey?"

"The cowgirls," I said.

"They pretty?"

"Yeah."

On Digging Deeper:

A SMALL QUEENSBRIDGE APPARTMENT *on the sixth floor of the blood-red brick projects complex right under the Queensborough Bridge in Long Island City, Queens. The kitchen, dining room, and living room were all linked together as one, only separated from a single bedroom in back by a dark, shadowy hallway.*

Laura slept on the couch, while I slept on a small cot in my parents' bedroom. Always sent to bed early, I fell off to sleep to the sounds of Peggy Lee on the Victrola or the Cisco Kid and Pancho on TV—compelled to fantasize about cowgirls riding their stallions across the bedroom walls.

Whatever couplings my parents could possibly have accomplished in that dark bedroom while I was supposed to be asleep were either partially remembered or—more often—simply repressed.

Chapter Three:
Subway to Coney

I WOKE UP FEELING BETTER. I knew I had the chance to go somewhere with Dad because he often took us out on Sundays, and I didn't want to spoil it by complaining. When I crawled out of bed and walked toward the bathroom, Dad was sitting on the can reading the baseball scores.

For most kids' fathers, studying baseball on the john might have been commonplace. And that alone might have completed the image. Not my dad. He'd sit there, his pants bunched down around his ankles, the newspaper spread out on his lap, a Camel drooping from his lip, a bag of chicharrones—deep fried pork rinds, his favorite delicacy—leaning against one leg, and a can of Pabst Blue Ribbon or Rheingold on the floor next to the other leg. And this morning was no different.

"Herman," Ma said, "get out of there."

"I'm enjoying life," he said. "If you don't enjoy it, it ain't worth living."

"Close the bathroom door then."

Dad just grunted.

"Herman, it's annoying. Close the door."

"You'll get used to it," Dad said. "I always do."

While I stood there, waiting, Mom just shook her head in disgust and gave Dad another dig:

"That doctor bill better get paid, mister."

There was that "mister" word again. No matter who said it, it seemed to carry a bit of family venom, as if to say, *listen to me when I'm talking. I mean this!*

"Yeah, yeah," Dad said, sarcastically. "It'll get paid. Or maybe we'll use the money to go to Arizona fa Joey's bronchitis." He looked at me and winked.

Mom had heard this nonsense before. She kept on walking toward the kitchen. As soon as she was out of earshot, Dad leaned over toward me and said:

"I don't like being closed in, Joe. I gotta be free."

I stood there in my pajamas, sleep still puffing up my eyes, my legs crossed in discomfort. But Dad just kept on talking.

"Ya heard the song by Cole Porter, 'Don't Fence Me In'? It reminds me of what California must be like."

Oh, give me land, lots a land,
Under starry skies above,
Don't fence me in.

"Wide-open space. No one to tell ya what to do. Someday we'll go there, Joey. It'll be good and dry for your lungs. And we'll go to the races and to the beach."

"Dad, I gotta go," I finally said.

"Yeah, we'll go, Joey, I promise. Land of freedom. California."

"No Dad, I really gotta go."

"C'mon, Joey, you can hold it."

HE PICKED UP HIS BEER and poured the rest of it down his open mouth, some of it splashing down his neck and shoulders and over the tattoo on his arm.

"Come into my office, Joey," he said. "But first, get me another beer."

"Please, Dad," I said, not caring if he accused me of complaining. If he was asking for another beer, it meant he'd be there for a while.

"Come on, Joey. Be a big boy."

So, I walked out to the kitchen to get Dad another beer. When Mom heard me coming, she opened the fridge, grabbed a bottle of Pabst and popped the cap.

"Here, give this to your father, he needs his breakfast," Mom said. "If he ever gets off, and he eventually will, you'll get to go. Soon, I promise.

"Who knows about the doctor bill," she went on. "And only God could know about Arizona. I mean California.

"I do know this: He'll get off the can before we ever get out of Queens."

Mom had been born in a cold-water flat in Hell's Kitchen, at 4248 28th Avenue, just off Ninth Street in Manhattan. She was one of seven kids who had all been born at home. Mom's parents, Laura Gaudiosi Gagliotti and Giovanni Gagliotti, had immigrated to New York in 1905 from a small town in southern Italy in the province of Basilicata. Years later, when I'd finally developed the interest and the courage to search for my roots, I discovered that they had been married in the small hill town of San Fele and fled their family, friends, and heritage not three weeks after their marriage. The reason? It was a secret no one ever found out about, even to this day.

A fact that was little known until I discovered it in 2008, over a hundred years after their emigration, was that my grandfather, Giovanni, had not come from San Fele at all, as was believed. He lived in a small peasant farm village about seventeen kilometers up the road. It seems likely that, as a day farm laborer who hired out to harvest grapes or wheat, Giovanni may have traveled to the fields below San Fele, where he met Laura who—I can only guess—may have been helping to feed the workers.

Not many people in my family were aware that my aunt Mary was born virtually nine months to the day after my grandparents' embarkation on the freighter Konigin Luise, which left from Naples on a November morning in 1905.

Aunt Mary was to be the first born in that house on 28th street. And my uncle Mike would be the last born, in 1924. In between, there would be six others: Margaret, Rose, Antonietta (or Annie, my mother), Millie, Nick, and Mike. These were the ones who survived. There were two other children, both named Philip, who did not survive to full adulthood. The first one died during childbirth, not a rare occurrence at that time. The second Philip, who had grown to young manhood, died in a car crash when he was twenty-one.

Years later, when I was born and my mother wanted to name me Philip, her mother told her that naming a boy Philip in our family would be a curse. My mother heeded the warning and named me Joseph.

Growing up in a family of eight children supported by a bootblack (yes, my own father started out as my maternal grandfather had) was not easy. Especially considering my grandfather's penchant for going to the tavern and buying a wooden bucket full of beer with his day's earnings, then coming home drunk and busted.

So, when Mom and her sister, Rose, met the two dashing Puerto Rican brothers, Herman and Johnny Ortiz, it was a way to flee from the family just as her parents had escaped their families in San Fele. The two couples were married a few years apart, two young and innocent sisters of Italian descent tying the marital knot with two handsome, crafty young Latin brothers.

I don't know how they got from Manhattan to Long Island

City. In those days, perhaps the neighborhoods of Queens looked like paradise to my father and his brother after fleeing the dank streets of San Juan in search of a better life. At least it must have appeared to be a way out of the sullen gloom of Hell's Kitchen. However it happened, both couples landed in connecting neighborhoods just across the Queensborough Bridge from Manhattan.

THAT MORNING, AFTER BREAKFAST Dad sat me on a phone book on the sofa, propped up my feet on a large can of Italian plum tomatoes, and started to shine my shoes.

He slapped his hand into the wax. Olive tan in color, his arms and hands looked like leather, the same shoe leather he was reputed to be such an expert at repairing. He spread the wax with his fingers—first rubbing them into the polish, then onto the shoes—building up a rhythm, like shadow boxing. When he used the brush, he worked it so hard my feet fell off the tomato can. He did the final buff with the canvas shoe rag, which snapped and popped in his alternating handiwork, as if he was punching with jabs and pauses, imitating Jersey Joe Walcott for me. As far as I knew, the snap and pop of the rag was the sound of leather meeting skin in a prizefight.

A few more jabs and pops and he came back yet again: "Wanna go to Coney Island to go fishing? We could getcha an ice cream cone, Joey. We could getcha a hot dog."

Without my even answering, he halted short and said, "Ya wanna go ta California?"

Before I could answer, he counter-punched, "Well, maybe we'll go ta California this winter." A few more pops of the rag and he stopped: "But maybe we'll go fishing today.

"Ya Mutha says we should go to Arizona someday. She thinks it'll be healthy for ya. And wouldn't you know it, California's not too far from there."

Dad lifted me off the pillow and stood me on my newly shined shoes.

Sure, I wanted to go fishing at the beach. But with Dad we never knew what we were in for. Would there be some glitch? Some so-called work Dad had to do? Would he ask us to be accomplices in one of his crazy schemes? Would he take us for a long subway ride, only to realize that he'd forgotten his money and we'd have to turn right around and go back home? One time that happened with a ballgame for Laura, who told me she always wondered if Dad knew the game was at the Polo Grounds in the Bronx instead of at Ebbits Field in Flatbush, and only took her to get away from Mom.

Later that morning Dad wrapped two battered, 10-inch-long tree branches with fishing lines, leaving a bit of a "handle," so we could hold on with one hand and throw the hook, bait, and sinker end with the other. Instead of those cool lead sinkers to weight our line, Dad used tobacco bags filled with sand. He found the old, cruddy sticks in the alley behind the shoe shop, so Laura and I didn't expect much. We felt odd and slightly abused at having to carry those contraptions on the subway, but we were still excited to get out of the projects.

Even back then the subway stop at Queensborough Plaza looked like a grotesque, steam-punk space station, serving several lines heading off in different directions. Once we caught the BMT line and Dad became distracted trying to look up a woman's dress, Laura leaned over to me and said, "Maybe this time we'll actually get our lines in the water."

The train—the same elevated subway we took out to Flushing to visit Aunt Margie and Uncle Frank—pulled out of the station, and soon after, we could see the happy Sunshine Baker waving to us from atop the Sunshine Bakery, a big brick building with millions of windows reflecting the morning sun. You'd think it would have been impossible to smell anything baking above the odors of the trains, buses, cars, and trucks, and all the surrounding factories. But the soft, sweet aroma of baked bread and Hydrox cookies rose above the city, making us feel like nothing bad could ever happen to us.

Soon, we got off that first train to change lines. Little did we know, but the trip would take us eight subway changes. So, we rode and stopped and caught another train. Then we did it all again. Like with the aspirin, I stopped counting after I got up to seven fingers. Laura and I started to get fidgety, so Dad launched into a story that gave him the captive audience that would slowly bring him out of his Sunday hangover and us out of the agony of the long ride.

"Lotta people think I'm the smartest shoemaker in New York, Laura," he said.

"Grimy Eddie comes in last week wit a pair a fifty-dolla shoes, wit a knife cut across the toe. Dey're wasted and nobody can use 'em. So, I talk him inta givin' me ten dollas to repair them. That's almost enough fa Joey's doctor bill."

As the train slowed down and pulled into the station at Coney, Laura whispered, "Daddy always ends a story at the good part—the stuff Mom doesn't want us to hear."

Dad marched us past the hot dog stands; past the rides, the colorful shops with Kewpie dolls and oversized Teddy bears, the stacked leaded milk bottles you had to knock over with battered baseballs. Breezing right by all the color and excitement, Dad walked swiftly ahead of us, constantly looking back, saying, "Come on kids, get going."

Laura saw the disappointment on my face. "Nevermind," she said. "Don't even ask. This is Coney, but you and I are going fishing. There's no money for all this good stuff."

When we finally arrived at the beach, Dad dragged us down to a bait shop, where he forked up 15 cents for a bag of live anchovies. My sister and I perked up. Dad had never gone this far before. Maybe we were really here to fish.

Eventually, far from the boardwalk, we walked out halfway onto the pier and Dad threw down our gear. He baited up our lines and heaved them out into the sun-speckled ocean, and said, "You kids wait here and fish for a while. I'll be right back."

"Okay," Laura said, "We'll be right here." She must have known from the tone of his voice and her teenage wisdom that Dad would be gone for a while, but I was in a vivid dream. Fishing. At the beach.

After a few hours, I got bored and started throwing rocks, shells, and bottle caps into the ocean to see if I could hit one of those million glittering specks of light reflecting off the water.

"Joey, will ya stoppit?" Laura said. "You're scaring away all the fish."

"How d'ya know?" I said.

"Well, you don't see any of them biting do ya?"

After sitting there quiet, motionless for what seemed like hours, and without feeling so much as a nibble, I realized we were alone.

"Where's Daddy?" I asked Laura.

"He's over at the bar near the station, having a beer with his friends," she said. "So shut up and pay attention to your line."

"But I thought we were going fishing," I told her. "I thought Daddy was taking us to the beach to go fishing."

"Well, we're at the beach," she said, staring out into the speckled, glittering ocean herself, never once looking at me.

"And we're fishing, aren't we?"

The dark and mysterious Italian side of the family . . .

AN OMEN, A CURSE, A "BAD EYE" *(mal occhio) kept watch over us—always lingering behind the stories.*

My mother's father, Giovanni Gagliotti, carried that sinister spirit with him as an angry peasant farmhand who, in the dark of night, left the small village of Atella in Basilicata in 1905 with his betrothed, Laura Gaudiosi, from the village of San Fele, 17 kilometers away. When relatives mentioned where the family had come from, they would only answer San Fele, then go silent, never mentioning Atella. Many relatives would hint that there was some secret they couldn't tell us.

Once the family had settled in America, my grandfather's iron hand ruled over my mother's early life and those of her six siblings in Hell's Kitchen, perhaps casting an indelible shadow over her own future life. Can it be said that she gravitated toward my father as a husband and soulmate out of childhood habit?

Does an abused daughter seek familiarity in an abusive husband?

Don't these look like shoes? Trust me, if the
photo were in color, it would look more
appetizing. But in a shoe repairman's
life, braciola *and shoes had a lot in common!*

Chapter Four:
Braciola and Eddie's Shoes

WE WAITED AND WAITED. By then Laura and I were cold and shivering, and the sun was fading toward New York; we weren't even fishing anymore. Laura said that, by the way Dad had talked, she wouldn't be surprised if he hadn't left for Miami and the dog races, or maybe we'd hear from him in a few weeks from Arizona or even California. At this news I felt myself becoming numb, starting to shiver even more.

As the evening became darker, a figure walking toward us on the pier came closer, and we could tell it was Dad because of his familiar swagger, whistling as if nothing had happened.

We started clawing at him, asking questions, but he didn't listen. He just said, "Pack up, kids, let's go." Laura knew what was happening. We were going to sit at a bar while Dad drank beer and yakked with his friends. If nothing else, we'd be out of the cold, and maybe he'd buy us glasses of coke with ice and cherries on top. And maybe we'd get in on a few more stories.

On the way to Sal's Bar, Dad started talking about the crap game again.

"The game always takes place in the alley behind the shoe shop, kids," Dad said.

"Eddie trows da dice and they land next to his new cordovan

49

French-toed shoes, and we all see a two-inch knife cut right on the toe.

"Eddie said they cost him fifty dollars at a shop on Lexington Avenoo. And when he said it happened in Harlem everyone gasped. It's a miracle to come back from Harlem with shoes at all, kids. With all your limbs intact."

Laura and I stared at one another.

"People like us cause trouble in Harlem, kids." Laura told me later that it didn't matter if a Puerto Rican like Dad had olive-colored skin, he better watch out in Harlem. And for a whitie like Eddie it was even worse.

"Eddie and this darkie get to scuffing and punching," Dad said, ". . . when the guy pulls out a knife."

Laura's eyes were bugging out and I'm sure mine were too.

"Eddie sweeps dis guy's feet out from under him," Dad said. "And the darkie lunges wit da knife and slashes Eddie's shoe.

"Eddie made it outta Harlem wit his life, kids," Dad said. "But his shoes are dead. So, he decides ta bring 'em ova to my shoe shop ta see what magic I can do."

Dad waited for a response from us, but we were speechless.

"Eddie said he wished da guy had cut his leg instead," Dad said. "Can you imagine? He was almost in tears."

Dad was getting to the good part just as we arrived at Sal's Place near the Boardwalk. When we walked in, Uncle Johnny and his daughter Rosemarie were sitting at the bar. But Johnny was too busy telling everyone he could make braciola even better than most Italians to even notice us.

"A lotta people think they know how ta make brasho," Uncle said. "But all kina people told me my brasho's da best.

"The secret is ta use all raw ingredients ta roll up in da beef. But I don't use no hard-boiled egg."

Everyone used to laugh at him until they tasted his braciola. Rosemarie started to say something about the egg, but Uncle

Johnny said, "Shut up, Rose, don't tell nobody my secret." Laura and I laughed; it was good to see someone else get told to shut up. Still, no one noticed us because Dad was practically holding us hostage by the door so we could hear the whole story.

"Da trouble wit the way da Dagos make it is using cooked egg," Uncle said. "But I use raw egg. Dat way, when you bake it, the egg doesn't dry out. And the meat doesn't taste like shoe leather.

"And speaking of shoe leather," Johnny said, lifting his glass and spotting Dad in the corner. "There's my brotha now, the best goddamn shoe repairman in the greata New York area."

Laura, Rosemarie, and I, now seated together at the bar, began to perk up when Johnny started talking about fixing shoes instead of food.

"Last week, during the crap game," Johnny said, "Herman proves he's da greatest. Eddie's got a cut on da toe of his shoe as wide as a darkie smilin' in the night. And Herman's da only shoe repairman in da greata New York area dat has da cajones to try and fix it. But it's gonna cost Eddie 20 bucks.

"Herman doesn't wanna give away no secrets. But I seen him do it before. He takes ground shoe leather, mixes it with cordovan shoe dye, some special glue, and rubs it inta da crack. Den he takes da filling down to the surface on the sanding wheel, buffs it out, and re-dyes the front tip of da shoe. Da naked eye can't tell da shoe's been touched. Like wit our cookin', da Puerto Rican mind can turn shit inta gold.

"It costs Herman 50 cents to do the job and he makes twenty bucks on da deal.

"But you're gonna die when you hear what happened next. . ."

"Now, Johnny," Dad said. His face turned that pale, pasty shade it got when he wound up in hot water with Mom. Uncle just kept on talking.

"When Eddie gets his hands on the dice," Uncle said, "Strange numbas start showing up. Eddie's numbas.

"Da pot grows," Uncle Johnny said. "Four, eight, sixteen, dollas. Herman starts ta turn blue.

"Pretty soon Eddie's twenty dollas up, and da twenty dollas Herman just talked outta Eddie ta fix da shoes are right back in Eddie's pocket."

ON THE SUBWAY HOME, a pretty lady across from us had her skirt hiked up. I looked over at Dad, whose head was cocked back, his mouth wide open. He must have fallen asleep while taking a look. Laura was distracted by playing with the fishing lines, so I leaned back and slid down in my seat to get my own look up the lady's skirt.

When we arrived at the elevated Queensborough station and went down to street level, we entered the Asian fish market, where Dad bought a few flounder filets. Outside the shop, he ripped off the white butcher paper and wrapped the fish in newspaper.

"Mom asks, we caught this offa da pier," he said. "It's fa her I'm doin' it. You know she gets sad when we don't catch no fish," he said. "She doesn't ask, don't say nothin'."

"And Eddie's shoes? Keep ya mouths shut."

A FEW DAYS AFTER Uncle Johnny described his recipe at Sal's bar, he showed Rosemarie and me how he made it the same way he and Dad told us about their antics—as if they knew the secret was safe with us because we were just kids.

Nobody knew Johnny's secret, even Aunt Rose. For some reason these peasants always harbored secrets. Like grandpa not wanting to talk about how or why he and his betrothed, Laura Gaudiosi, left Basilicata; like Dad and Johnny not talking about how their experience with their father led to their escaping San Juan for New York, no one ever wanted to talk about it. Still we kids always tried everything we could to make sense of it all.

Legs:

MY FATHER TAUGHT ME HOW TO LOOK UP WOMEN'S SKIRTS. *His teaching may not have been intentional: I learned by observation.*

On long subway rides to Coney Island he'd ride slouched low, his mouth agape, his head tilted to one side, his eyes half shut as if asleep or recovering from last night's bender on Rheingold beer and Camel straights.

But he'd had his eyes open all along.

One Sunday on a train to Ebbits Field, he looked up and saw me glaring at him. He perked up, pumped his eyebrows at me and nodded toward the lady across from us and smiled as if to say, "Don't give us away."

There it was, the beautiful creamy thigh above the stockings, wonderful for us to look at.

Laura, seven years older and wise to our game, would shake her head at us, knowing what Dad was up to. Years later she confirmed that he taught us bad habits simply through his bad behavior— silently, as if he were telling us, "Watch what I can do."

After all these years, it haunts me as the first thing I look at in women. Not an eye, a face, a smile, an essence. But legs. Slowly I've come to know we live out the habits we've learned in childhood— good, bad, playful, or controlling.

Well into early adulthood, I began to dread my obsession with this compulsion. But I wrote it off as the wound of misplaced child-hood mimicry rather than what it must have been: the influence of a narcissistic father who felt he could do anything he damned well pleased and get away with it.

Chapter Five:
Freddie's Offer and Pasta Fazool

LAURA ALWAYS WANTED TO GET RID OF ME—and go on her merry way—after picking me up from school. So, when we got to the corner on our way home from P.S. 111, she would shove me along 40th Avenue toward the shoe shop, where the vinegary aroma of ground leather and shoe dye pulled me in by my nose.

One day, Dad was standing at the counter talking to a lady about a pair of shoes with a broken buckle, flipping it with his finger as if it were a scab about to come off a scrape on your knee.

"I don't know if I can fix dis," Dad said. He shook his head, made the "tisk, tisk, tisk" sound, and flashed her an indignant look that said, You bring me this petty little crap? What a waste of my time. Dad told me later that the sour look on his face was intended to set the customer up to think the job was difficult, if not impossible.

"I could try something I learned in Puerto Rico," he said. "But I can't guarantee nothing." Now he had her. Her face turned glum. By making it sound like some trick he'd learned in the jungle outside San Juan using hemp and natural glue made from the sap of a special tree, Dad could make a customer think no one else could do the job. Resigned, the lady agreed that it was better to risk some kind of ethnic cure than to buy a new pair of shoes.

"Five dollas," Dad said.

She gasped. So, Dad flashed her a sarcastic smile. He slid the shoes back across the counter, folded his arms, and said nothing. She pondered a minute. She handed them right back to Dad.

"Here," she said, scurrying toward the door. "Do your magic. I need them by Saturday."

As the woman left, Freddie the bookie came into the shop, sliding around the doorway like a cartoon character slithering across a movie screen.

Dad's demeanor changed immediately. He became timid in a way that suggested, had the woman with the broken buckle still been there, he surely would have offered to do the job for fifty cents. Freddie's arrival caused the veins on Dad's arms to throb; they changed from Puerto Rican blue to a vivid shade of magenta.

"Uh . . . Freddie," Dad said. "Dat fourteen dollas I owe ya is . . ."

"Don't worry, Herman," Freddie said.

"Wha . . . wha?" Dad said. I'd never seen him speechless.

"The shoes in the window, Herman. The cordovan French-toes?"

"The guy never showed up," Dad said. "He owes me twenty dollas fa doze mutha f . . ." Dad stopped when he noticed me crouched in the corner listening.

"Wait, Freddie," Dad said. "I'm going to give Joey some lunch in the back room. Then we can talk.

"Come on, Joey," he said to me. "Ya supposed ta eat. We're gonna be here late tonight. Here's ya mother's pasta fagioli."

"FAGIOLI?" Freddie roared, grabbing the bag from Dad. "It's Pasta Fazool. That's what we call it in Sicily." He opened the container and sniffed inside the lid, his face turning sour at the aroma.

"And don't forget, you gotta soak the beans ovanight. Otherwise . . . you know," he said, wrinkling up his nose.

"You start with onions and garlic, diced carrots, and celery, and cook it so it's nice and brown. That's what makes the flava. That's-a goo'."

Just then Laura walked in, her catcher's mitt buckled to her belt, her dungarees rolled up to her shins, her two fire-engine-red pigtails dangling from under her Dodgers cap.

She sneered out of her chewing-gum-smacking mouth:

"What's he taukin' 'bout? He thinks he knows how ta make soup? Dad, ain't you gonna stick up fa Ma? Mama's fagioli's the best."

Dad raised his open hand toward her and waved her toward the back. Oblivious to the rigamarole of our family exchange, Freddie went on. "Most people don't realize you gotta brown the vegetables . . . "

"We know that, Freddie," Dad said, interrupting.

Freddie just glared at Dad. So Dad shut up.

We all realized we were going to hear what we didn't want to hear: an entire ethnic discourse on what creates flavor in soup. From a bookie. A loan shark. A guy who can make you regret questioning his mother's cooking.

"If you brown the vegetables," Freddie said, "you can get the flav' of meat, which is at a premium in a country like Sicily."

Laura told me later that she and Dad knew that Sicily wasn't its own country, but they didn't dare say anything.

"You used all the tricks you could to give your soup a meaty flav'," Freddie said. "I'm not saying we were poor and couldn't afford no meat, just that my family didn't spend money when they didn't have to."

Laura and Dad were still listening. But I got bored, so I went over to the window and started flicking the shoelaces on the cordovan shoes that had already caused so much fear and fable in our family saga. As I flicked the laces the same way Dad had flicked the buckle on the lady's shoes, Freddie came over and grabbed the shoes right from under my hands.

"You know you owe me fourteen dollas, and you know I can call it due any time, Herman," Freddie said, "I want these shoes."

Dad went catatonic. Laura and I knew the story and it was getting thick as pasta fazoo.

"But Freddie," Dad said. "I was gonna make twenty dollas fa fixing doze shoes. Da money was fa Joey's docta bill."

"Look, I'll set the fourteen dolla debt to rest. Plus, I'll give you ten more. You're half-way home."

"I don't know, Freddie."

"Herman," Freddie said, putting his hand up to his chest, caressing something inside his coat and shaking his head.

"No, No, Freddie," Dad said, starting to talk real fast. "I wasn't saying I wouldn't take the deal. It's just . . . look at these heels." Dad held the shoes up for Freddie to see.

"I wouldn't feel right," Dad said. "Let me put on new ones. I'll trow it in fa nothin'."

Freddie smiled. He pulled his hand away from whatever he was fondling in his jacket. Laura and I looked at one another.

So far nothing had been said about the ugly scar that used to appear across the toe of the left shoe. Would Freddie's offer have been so generous if he knew about the scar? Also, Dad was being careful not to mention that the shoes belonged to Eddie. How was he going to get around that?

Freddie agreed to let Dad keep the shoes to fix them up since he saw that the heels were a little worn, and he knew he'd now be getting something he hadn't bargained for. Dad always said that Sicilians liked favors; they liked to be indebted to one another. Their family code and sense of values was based on trading intimate favors, taking care of their own.

As Freddie made his way toward the door, the three of us

silently sighed now that the encounter was over. But then he turned and looked at Dad.

"You know, Herman," Freddie said. "I've been looking for Grimy Eddie Ryan. Have you seen him?"

We all got squeamish again. It wasn't over after all.

"He's outta town," Dad said. "I haven't seen him in weeks."

"You sure, Herman?"

The atmosphere was getting thick again. Dad had no reason to lie this time. It was really true. Only there were so many rumors floating around about the shoes that we thought Freddie's question might uncover something unhealthy for Dad.

"Why you looking for him?" Dad said.

"He owes me. I decided this wormy little Irish kid's gotta have his arm broken for him, to teach him a lesson."

"Kids," Dad said. "Go inta the backroom."

We walked off slowly, because we wanted to hear the rest of the story. And as long as we were moving, Dad didn't notice that we were still just inching our way toward the back.

"Dat's a pretty serious thing ta axe," Dad said. "I was wondering if maybe . . . " Dad paused.

"What, Herman?" Freddie said. "You know something?"

"Well, I thought you might be able to send another twenty dollars my way fa some information," Dad said. "I'm not trying to squeeze you, Freddie. Don't get me wrong. But if I'm fixing those shoes fa you, I'm still gonna be short on Joey's doctor bill and . . ."

"Okay, Herman, look, you got the extra twenty . . . As long as you can tell me something about Eddie that I can use to square up with him."

By now Laura and I were right behind the curtain that separated the back room from the front of the shop. We were leaning over, gripping one another, trying to hear what was going to happen next. We wondered how Dad was going to get the shoes back from Eddie, and how he was going to buy more time to make the pieces of this crazy puzzle fit together.

Dad leaned over near the door toward Freddie and said, "Eddie is going to be right here in the back alley on Satedy night. He's promised to make it to the crap game. It's always over at midnight because that's when Johnny and I go to the Copa for salsa dancing."

Dad told Freddie everything he wanted to know. So, Freddie reached in his pocket, pulled a big wad of bills. "Hold out ya hand, Herman."

Dad held out his hand. Freddie peeled off a crisp 20-dollar bill and handed it to Dad. "Dats fa da shoes."

Dad smiled even more. Freddie counted out fourteen dollars . . . and Dad really started to smile then. But Freddie stopped. He took the fourteen dollars back. "You owe me that fourteen, Herman."

Nevertheless, Dad was still excited. He mumbled a few words, probably thanking Freddie, but we couldn't hear what he said.

Then he told Freddie he'd get the shoes ready for him: new heels, a new shine, even some new laces. But he didn't say one word about the fact that when Eddie came to the shoe shop on Saturday night, he'd be coming for the express purpose of picking up his cordovan French-toed shoes.

Truth or fiction ?

How far does a story have to go *off the truth of what really happened before it's considered fabrication?*

Most writers build a story, real or fictional, out of events that are strung together in an unfolding narrative. The fiction writer shapes a story as a full-blown fabricated tale, while the memoirist attempts to convey truthfully-remembered occurrences as a string of related events—dutifully adding the connective tissue of invented narrative glue to paste it all together.

For half-remembered experiences, the memoirist relies on stories told and re-told around the kitchen table, photographs, and accompanying anecdotes that explained them, shards of gossip heard down on the block that lead a child to reconstruct a mythical armature of what "might have happened."

This form of re-fabrication helped me as a child to make sense of what I may have been forced to repress. Can it be that we, as abused children, can't bear to face the real thing that happened, so we build a fictional story out of it? Perhaps burnishing it with humor, deflection, and the amber patina of childhood hope—wishful remembering?

In a good memoir, readers feel assured that the events did happen. But there is always the cloud of uncertainty about what a child can and can't remember.

Maybe novels and short stories—like the improvised, half-remembered connective tissue of memoir—are merely disguised past experiences re-imagined in fabricated situations with invented characters in sheep's clothing.

In this way I see memoir as a more truthful form of fiction. Even though we're forced to bend the truth a bit.

Chapter Six:
Eddie Arrives from Boca Raton

THANK GOD FREDDIE FINALLY LEFT. We were famished from the aggravation he stirred up in our stomachs. Only a taste of Mom's good pasta fagioli would satisfy our hunger and quell our nerves.

Dad came looking for us behind the curtain, where he probably thought we were goofing off. Did he care that we had heard the rest of the story about Freddie, Eddie, and the shoes?

"Come on, kids," Dad said. "Let's set the table. Ya mutha put her whole heart and soul inta dis pasta fagioli. I don't care what Freddie calls it, or how his mother makes it."

Dad had a hot plate in the back that he used for making special glue. He dusted out a pot to use for heating the soup. He pulled down some silverware, paper napkins, and bowls that he kept on a shelf in the back room just for such occasions: dinner at the shoe shop while Mom was visiting Aunt Margie in Flushing. He set up the card table hidden behind the curtain. Laura and I sat with our backs to the front door so Dad could sit looking out, in case any customers showed up.

Just as we started to dig in, we heard the doorbell jingle. When Dad looked up, his face turned as white as one of Mom's fresh laundered sheets and he said, "Jesus Christ."

Laura and I dropped our spoons and turned around. It was

Grimy Eddie Ryan walking into the shop—suntanned, dressed in a white Panama hat and a cream-colored linen suit. He was all smiles.

"Hey, Herman," he yelled.

Dad jumped up and grabbed Laura and me by the shoulders. He squeezed real hard and said, "You kids stay in here and eat." We could tell he really meant it, so we dug back into our soup.

"Eddie," Dad said. "Fa chrissakes, I thought you were going ta be in Miami until Satedy."

"I got lucky, Herman," Eddie said. Laura and I looked at one another. There was that word "lucky" showing up again in the most unlikely places.

"I won the Exacta down at St. Petersburg Park," Eddie said.

"Three races in a row!" Dad said. "That's a small fortune."

We could hear Eddie getting excited. He must have pulled out a wad of money and started flashing it at Dad, because we could hear the shuffling of bills, and Dad was starting to react with the snorts and giggles he made when he returned from the track a winner.

Then Dad changed his tune.

"But Eddie," Dad said. "Dis could be dangerous."

Laura nudged me and silently mouthed the word Freddie.

"Herman?" Eddie said, with a blank stare.

Dad rebounded. "Uh . . . well, all that money. You better not be flashing that stuff around. And ya shoes, I never had a chance . . ."

"Never mind," Eddie said. "Look at these two-toned oxfords I picked up in Boca Raton."

As Eddie looked down at his feet, Dad leaned over the counter to peer at Eddie's new shoes. While they both oohed and ahhed, Dad reached behind his back, grabbed the cordovan French-toes from the shelf and put them under the counter where Eddie couldn't see them.

"Well, I figure you still want 'em, right?"

"Yeah, sure," Eddie said. "But I'm not in a hurry."

"Well, Eddie, since you're flush," Dad said. "Maybe you could float me a few more bucks to put heels on 'em. When you get 'em back dey might as well be perfect. What d'ya thin'?"

"Okay," Eddie said. He reached back into his pocket, peeled off a five-dollar bill and threw it at Dad. "Will that cover it?"

After Eddie walked out and we heard the door slam, Dad came in back with the crisp new five-dollar bill clenched between his teeth. He walked over to us like a bigshot, swaggering and holding out his arms like a tightrope walker at Ringling Brothers. He opened his mouth and the bill floated down to the table.

"Kids," he said. "Ya fatha's a genius."

Laura and I were beginning to think that Dad really was a genius. He had just sold the same heel job twice. Everyone was throwing money at him. He was such a fast talker that nobody could keep track of what was going on. But if he was so slick and smooth, then why was Mom always yelling at him about money? And would he be able to stay one step ahead of the game? How would he bend and squirm when both Eddie and Freddie showed up wanting the same pair of shoes?

As we dug into the pasta fagioli and started to moan over the rich, soothing flavor of Mom's soup, Dad said: "Well kids, ya father's finally startin' ta have some luck."

There was that word again.

THE DAY AFTER EDDIE got back from Boca Raton in his new Oxford shoes, his cream-colored suit, and his sublime ignorance about the fact that Freddie was on the lookout for him, Mom and I were the only ones home as the ringer washing machine gyrated and sloshed in the hallway by the bathroom.

She was making ravioli and, at the same time, keeping one

eye on me and the other on the wash. Occasionally, she'd run from the kitchen, then to the wringer washing machine, which in its gyrations marched like a soldier, advancing on an enemy. Could the enemy eventually be me?

In the kitchen Mom juggled three things for the "ravis"—the dough, the filling, and the sauce.

For the dough she made a big mound of flour in the middle of the table and hollowed out a well in the center of the mound. She cracked a couple of eggs into the well, along with a few tablespoons of milk. Then she whipped up the eggs with the fingers of one hand and swirled them around the well to pick up the flour. The swirling of the eggs was hypnotic. "Like scrambled eggs, Ma?" I said.

"Yeah, Joey, ya fatha's whole life is like scrambled eggs. *Uovua strapazzate.*" At the time it went right over my head.

When Mom got the eggs and flour in a shaggy mass, she kneaded it on the table—but not too long, because you didn't want the dough to become too elastic or it would spring back awkwardly while trying to roll it out and the finished pasta would be tough to the bite.

Just then Laura walked in and threw her books on the table. She always knew when Mom finished kneading the dough. She went into the kitchen and grabbed off a pinch, put it into her mouth and started to chew. Mom grabbed her by the ear, walked her over to the sink, and told her to spit it out. But Laura just swallowed. She pulled up Mom's apron, twirled her around madly while humming a tarantella until Mom squealed with delight and begged Laura to stop. Still spinning, Mom tried to grab Laura by one of her pigtails, but it was too late. Laura had already ducked under Mom's arms, grabbed another piece of the dough, and ran out to meet her friends to sing doo-wop on the corner.

When Mom regained her breath, she settled in to make the

filling: Ricotta cheese, grated Parmesan, an egg, some chopped parsley, and a dash of salt and pepper. Then Mom yelled, "Be careful the filling isn't too wet, or it'll soak through the dough when the ravis go into boiling water to cook." You can always add a little more Parmesan to dry out a wet filling, and dry is always better than wet, "or they'll get mushy."

While the dough relaxed—allowing it to become homogeneous and pliable—Mom went out to do a load of wash. So, I tagged along, in rhythm to the sway and swish of the washing machine, mesmerized by the ringers as they rolled and rolled. The fun began when the wash was done, and Mom sent each garment through the ringer to squish out the water.

After the ravioli dough had relaxed under the damp towel for half an hour, Mom cut off a piece and started to roll it out on a well-floured table. If the dough was too elastic and kept springing back, she'd let it rest a few more minutes. It was hard to get it to the proper thickness by just rolling it, so occasionally Mom would roll the dough onto the rolling pin, drape it over the edge of the table and s-t-r-e-t-c-h the dough. All the while the washing machine kept swirling.

When the dough was in a large rectangle, Mom used a tablespoon to place dollops of the filling a few inches apart across its length. Then she folded the dough over the filling dollops, creating a strip of dough with lumps. Some people think you must brush the dough with water before you fold it over so it will stick. But Mom said no, not if your dough was moist (and not overly floured) so it would stick together at the folds.

Mom used the edge of her hand to press channels between the lumps of filling. With a zigzag rolling wheel, she cut each ravi into a large square. Then she pricked them with a fork to make sure they wouldn't balloon up with air when boiled. Finally, she carried several at a time, using her upturned apron, into the bedroom and placed them on a flour-dusted sheet to dry.

As I drifted back and forth, following Mom, I could see and hear the throbbing and sloshing of the machine as it marched back and forth in the hall, those two grey, ominous rubber rollers—rolling, rolling, as I passed—reminding me of the rolling pin Mom used to roll the dough.

I was mesmerized. The rollers seemed like big, welcoming lips, so I stood up on tiptoes and reached my hand up to feel them roll, when my fingers got nipped. At first, I started to laugh; it was thrilling. But then, the rubber lips began to gobble up my fingertips until my hand was halfway into the rollers. The big, ugly machine was now starting to lift me up off the floor. It started to swallow me—first my hand, then my forearm. Then my elbow. And my arm began to s-t-r-e-t-c-h. I started to feel like the ravioli dough when Mom slung it over the table to stretch it thinner. When I was up to my elbow, the machine began to whine and wail. I screamed for Mom. It was more of a shriek. I was being eaten alive.

Mom ran in from the kitchen and saw me up to my shoulder in the rollers and she shrieked even louder than I had. She dropped her rolling pin and ran toward me and grabbed my body to relieve the tension on my arm. But she couldn't release the ringer with just one hand, so she let go of me and quickly spun the red twist handle on top of the ringer that locks the rollers in place.

Once it was released, I fell to the floor like a wet and twisted Turkish towel.

It was time for Mom to call Doctor Boccardi again. In my mind, I imagined the taste of aspirin.

ONE OF MY MOTHER'S primary jobs was to soothe my pain, bandage my bruises, dry my tears. This she did with the same dedication that any mother would bring to the role. It just seemed like she was doing it all the time.

That day the ravioli sat. The laundry went undone; the washing machine stood silent. Mom fondled me in a blanket on her lap and rocked me in her arms until I stopped crying. Then she got up and called Dr. Boccardi, who rushed right over.

Again, it seemed traumatic at the time, and when Mrs. Vynella came over, she said, "It's a good thing a kid's bones are like rubber. If that happened to a grownup, you'd probably have to cut off their arm."

"ANGIE, PLEASE!!" Ma said.

When Boccardi left, everything was okay again, even though my arm felt like it was wrenched out of its socket. I had a throbbing pain in my elbow and shoulder. And just as the doctor left, he handed Mom a piece of paper. This time it wasn't a prescription because all he said I needed was some aspirin—the universal cure. The piece of paper was a reminder that another six-dollar house visit would be added to my bill.

Resigned, Mom cuddled me up in the same old blanket on the couch and went in to cook some ravis. I couldn't see her from the couch, but I had watched her many times before: You gently drop a few ravis in a large pot of salted boiling water. When they float to the top, they're done.

"Make sure the edges are cooked," I yelled to Ma from my perch on the couch. It was one important thing I'd remembered her telling me.

"Yeah, Yeah, Joey. Sure," she said.

Remove them with a slotted spoon, drain them in a colander, put three or four on a plate, cover them with a little tomato sauce and Parmesan. And eat.

Oh, I forgot to mention the sauce. It's simple. Fry up some chopped garlic in fruity olive oil until it's pale. Open a couple cans of whole pear tomatoes and drain off the liquid, then squeeze out the seeds. Add the tomatoes to the olive oil and garlic mixture; break them up and sauté them for several minutes.

Then add a little chopped oregano, parsley, or basil, some salt and pepper. Then leave it alone.

Or "nevermind."

"Nevermind" was what my family said when you weren't supposed to do anything else to something that's cooking: you just leave it alone, it's done already. You also said it when you'd be better off not thinking about something that was giving you aggravation. Like some pain in the neck someone was giving you. It was a little like "fagetaboutit," except fagetaboutit was more what the men said about gambling, money, and work, and "nevermind" was what the women said about cooking and taking care of the kids. And talking about a husband's bad habits.

Two similar phrases with two subtly different meanings. It was a little bit of peasant wisdom. And like Mom's soup, or the pasta that helped to soothe the pain of Dad's wicked life and all the stupid accidents I'd inflicted on myself, those two phrases got us through a lot of bad times.

Chaos as a troublesome fabric

CHAOS WAS ALL AROUND *during my childhood: people coming and going, conflicting stories about gambling and drunkenness. My father's habits. And it seems only natural that chaos, when encountered in present-day life, can make one relive a feeling that enveloped us in childhood.*

Writer Vivian Gornick says "we become what is done to us." Not only have we been shaped by what we've been exposed to; it can make us feel a certain way in adult life when we face similar situations. Add to that what Freud said: "we have a compulsion to repeat the bad behaviors we experienced in our past," endlessly hoping to conquer their hold on us. So, now I start to understand how past chaotic moments can complicate everyday living.

That realization can be soothing.

Now it's easier to cope whenever disturbing situations present themselves: dealing with the confusion of thoughts, remembrances, and experiences.

Calling up a feeling we once had can remind us that this is a new time. It takes a small step of courage and insight to realize that the present-day chaos does not have to bring on that old, debilitating feeling.

Can it just be recognized and then let go?

Chapter Seven:
The Crap Game of Eddie's Life

AT THE TIME NOBODY in the family but Dad knew what happened at the weekly crap game, because he never told anyone. Us kids weren't allowed to ask any questions or even bring it up. Especially around Mom. Eventually, we pieced together the story of that particular Saturday night from a few details cousin Rosemarie had heard Uncle Johnny telling Aunt Rose, and from tidbits Laura and I heard at the shoe shop later that week. Still other things may or may not have happened, so Laura and I made up stories to connect the insanity of what we knew. We felt guilty because we were following Dad's example by lying about events in order to make things turn out the way we wanted them to. But as far as we could figure out, this is what happened:

It was a few minutes before 8:00 on Saturday night, just before Dad was scheduled to close the shop. He was sweeping up and emptying the garbage cans when he heard a knock at the door. Dad had already flipped over the open/closed sign, so you can be sure he wasn't about to open the door for anyone. He looked out from behind the back curtain and saw that it was Freddie.

Dad ducked down and hid. Most of the trusted stories we heard suggested that he was on his knees starting to pray. Now, everyone who knew my father understood that things had to be pretty bad for him to have anything to do with the Father, the Son, OR the Holy Ghost, besides taking one of their names in vain. Eventually, Dad gathered his courage. He got up, went over to the window by the door to greet Freddie when, across the street, he saw a Checkered Taxi pull up; Eddie got out and started to pay the cabbie. And Dad panicked.

"Freddie," Dad said. "I can't let you in. If I open the door, the alarm will go off."

"It's okay," Freddie whispered and hunkered down too so he wouldn't be noticed. "I'm leaving, I just want to pick up my shoes. But, by the way, Herman, how you gonna get out?"

Dad had to think fast. "I get out through the back window. The landlord's supposed ta get this damn thing fixed any day now."

"The back window," Freddie said. "You're crazy, Herman. I'm watching you."

"I know."

"And my shoes?"

"The new heels will be done early next week," Dad said. "But promise me something, Freddie. Don't break Eddie's arm during the game. It would look bad, you know? The last time something like that happened I had to close the game for a month."

"Break his arm?" Freddie said. "Ha. Ha. I'll be back."

"Yeah," Dad said. "Now get outta here, willya? If I don't pull the safety switch within five minutes, the alarm goes off. And I can't stop it without the cops coming."

Just the mention of cops made Freddie disappear.

Across the street, Eddie finished paying the cabbie and started walking toward the shoe shop in his new summer outfit. He saw Herman in the window, so he waved to him and pointed toward the corner as if to say, "I'll meet you around back."

That night the crap game took place as scheduled in the back alley. The usual participants—Uncle Johnny, Eddie, my father, and a couple Italians from the neighborhood—were joined by one of Eddie's Irish friends, who brought the whiskey.

Because Eddie was a big roller when he had extra cash, he became impulsive with his wagers. My father started winning. But as usual when he grabbed the dice, he started to bet impulsively too. And his luck changed. It took him three-and-a-half hours to win seventy-five dollars from Eddie, and in 20 minutes his winnings dwindled down to the 35 he had started with—what Eddie had originally advanced him to fix the shoes.

The game was almost over. You could tell Eddie was relieved at getting some of his money back. So Dad just blurted out what was on his mind.

"Listen, Eddie," Dad said. "I'll give you the thirty-five dollars back if you let me keep the shoes."

Eddie stood there for a moment, speechless.

"Explain this to me, Herman," Eddie said. "You'll never fit into my shoes. Why would you want them?"

"I'm embarrassed, Eddie," Dad said. "I can't even tell you, I'm so embarrassed."

Uncle Johnny quickly chimed in, and—as we were to find out later—he really didn't know what was going on. But seeing how Dad was acting and how he was pimping Eddie, Johnny knew that Dad was up to something. Furthermore, the two brothers were natural accomplices, having used the same one-two punch on suckers many times before.

"It's tragic, Eddie," Johnny said, ". . . when a guy like Herman can't do the magic wit someone's shoes like he promised." He raised his eyebrow at Herman. Then Dad went back at Eddie with a counter-punch.

"I couldn't pull it off," Dad said. "I can't even show you da shoes. It'd kill me. Forget the thirty-five dollars. Let's call it even. For me, Eddie. Please."

Eddie hated to see Dad break down like that. And he was pretty flush anyway, having won so much money at the track in Miami. He had bought himself a new suit, new shoes. And besides, he hated to lose the thirty-five. So he said okay.

The game always wound up at midnight. When it was over, and everyone else had gone, Herman and Johnny stood under the amber light of the lamppost that hangs over the alley. As they chuckled about putting one over on their Irish buddy, they both watched Eddie walk off toward his apartment located on Vernon Boulevard, near the East River, right under the Queensborough Bridge.

And as we learned later, that was where Eddie was last spotted by the hoboes that lived under the bridge tower—never to be seen again.

Could it be what the grownups were always talking about in the kitchen, but went silent when I walked in? Something about cement boots and a body being found in the East River?

Laura wouldn't explain it to me. And I didn't want to know.

The "cement buckets."

DID THAT TERRIFYING PHRASE REALLY MEAN what it sounded like? To a six-year-old: images of suffocation; deep pressure in one's chest; being unable to take in air under water.

Like that ever-swelling torrent of kids at the Silver Cup Bakery you're soon to hear about; like the gasping I experienced when Dad stormed into the bedroom to break my fever by breathing life into me.

The sensation of being held down, the nightmares triggered by the image of cement buckets. The fear of what that indescribable image could possibly mean.

Chapter Eight:
The Cisco Kid and Pancho at the Silvercup

IT WAS SUNDAY MORNING about a week after the big crap game. When I dragged myself out of bed, the house was quiet.

Laura and Mom were gone to early mass. As I walked down the hall in my pajamas, I heard voices and tinkling glasses from the kitchen, where Dad and Uncle Johnny were sitting at the table, drinking beers and eating lupini, Italian beans similar to fava beans or lima beans soaked in brine and served as an appetizer. The Puerto Rican brothers, just in from a night of salsa dancing, were doing what they'd learned from the Italian side of the family: biting off the tips of the skins and squeezing the insides into their mouths.

"So, Herman," Uncle said. "What you heard from Eddie?"

"Nothing," Dad said, popping lupini and washing them down with swigs of Rheingold. "Not one word. For all I know he's got a broken arm and he's lying low so Freddie will fagetabout 'im."

When I walked in, they both clammed up and Johnny said, "Ya goin' ta see Cisco and Pancho today, Joey?"

Herman and Johnny reminded me of my TV heroes, Cisco and Pancho, but without the horses and sombreros. When they were dressed for a night of dancing, they wore broad collared,

pinstriped suits—Dad's navy blue, Johnny's chocolate brown, their jet-black hair slicked straight back. My father was thin, handsome, streetwise, and crafty, and he always wanted to be in charge. With his occasional pencil-thin mustache, he looked just like Cisco. Uncle Johnny was the sidekick. Stout with an even thicker mustache, he always flashed a fiendish smile. And he would wink at you and pump his eyebrows—just like Pancho—as if you were able to understand what the hell he was gesturing about.

Still, just like Dad, Cisco and Pancho were my heroes.

When I heard that they were going to make a personal appearance at the Silvercup Bakery in Long Island City, Queens, I couldn't think of anything else until the day I would see them ride up on their horses.

The Silvercup factory was a dingy old building under the Queensborough Bridge. Silvercup Bread was their sponsor, but Laura and I could never quite figure out what a fluffy white bread had to do with two Mexican cowboys. Like Dad and Johnny, Cisco and Pancho never ate bread. Yet there they were—The Cisco Kid and Pancho, pushing a fluffy white bread at a hundred thousand multi-ethnic kids in Queens.

The only reason Mom let me go to the personal appearance without her was that Laura had agreed to take me, watch me, and never let me out of her sight. Had my mother ever anticipated how crazy it would get, she never would have let me go.

Laura and I arrived at the bakery along with a thousand screaming kids trying to squeeze themselves through the bakery's huge roll-down doors, the same doors that each morning spewed forth an endless caravan of trucks on their way to deliver bread, muffins, and crumb cakes to local stores. The mob of hysterical kids was pulsating rhythmically like a giant serpent. The minute we arrived, I wanted to be a part of the action. The magic of TV had imprinted on our minds an image of these two handsome caballeros in brightly embroidered outfits, their sombreros bouncing up and down as they rode. That day our heroes would be right in front of us, not just fuzzy images on a screen, nor a cluster of tiny black and white dots. Their skin, like Herman and Johnny's would have a romantic olive color instead of the lifeless gray of television. And they would speak to us . . . and sign autographs.

After we stood outside a few moments, Laura wanted to find the best way in, so she grabbed my hand real tight, looked me straight in the eye, and said:

"Joey, you wait here." How many millions of times had I heard that?

Then she let go of my hand, turned away, and left.

There I was alone. What Mom feared most. Now I knew why. I stood there for what seemed like forever, not moving an inch—when suddenly I was caught up in the wave of delirious kids streaming in through the big roll-down doors that looked like the mouth of a giant, hungry whale. In a moment, I was carried helplessly by this torrential wave of children, whose screaming delight only terrified me—my feet never touching the ground. Just when this human river went through another doorway, narrowing its wide swath to enter, the intensifying energy became uncontrolled, ferocious. I was pushed, pulled, bobbed up, and stuffed down into this churning river; then, one quick moment later, a sudden wave heaved me into the air and then back under, tossed and tumbled onto the dirty gray concrete floor, underneath a blur of stampeding feet. I was being trampled, suffocated. I tried to take a breath, but no air came in. I felt the river becoming an ocean as big as any in the world and tried desperately to lift my head above the raging torrent. My body was helpless, so my mind tried to escape, resort to some form of fantasy: think about my fairy cowgirls, rolling dice with Dad, the soothing saltiness of pastina—anything to help me "go away for a while," my typical reality-denying escape strategy. But no amount of mental fantasy would work.

I was trapped and I blacked out for what seemed like an eternity, drowning in a dark sea of amnesia.

But a miracle happened. Someone grabbed hold of my arm, lifting me out of the current. Now I floated on top of the wave of children instead of underneath it. When I came to and looked up, a teenage girl was holding my hand and pulling me out of the nightmare. Suddenly, it felt like a waterfall had burst over a cliff and emptied the turbulent river into a calm, safe pool.

I don't remember what happened after that. I can't recall if I found Laura, or she found me. I didn't care if I ever got a glimpse of Cisco and Pancho before they rode off. I didn't care if Laura saw them without me. I was glad to be alive.

As USUAL, THERE WAS FOOD waiting at home. No one could have guessed what had happened, so the cream pudding that Aunt Rose was stirring on the stove was merely a part of the everyday ritual of making some kind of treat for us kids. And Rose's recipe is so simple: two cups of milk, a half teaspoon of cornstarch, and three tablespoons of sugar, if my memory holds. Maybe a hint of vanilla.

As Aunt Rose stirred the Cream over medium heat, Mom noticed that I looked a little battered. She started to get worked up. Laura downplayed the whole thing, telling Mom I had "just gotten lost." Was that what happened? I wondered.

Rose's daughter, Cousin Rosemarie, who may have felt jealous that she hadn't been invited to see the Mexican cowboys, started acting up by pretending to hug Aunt Rose from behind as a ploy to reach around her and stick her finger in the Cream for a taste. Rose giggled, then slapped Rosemarie away. But as the Cream started to thicken and Aunt Rose yelled to us that it was almost ready, Mom continued to badger Laura about what had happened. Laura made it sound like it was my fault—that I had let go of her hand and didn't listen. Maybe part of that was true. So, I didn't argue; that might have forced me to talk about it, and Mom might find out the entire story. Instead, I squealed along with Rosemarie to Aunt Rose for a plate of the Cream.

After Mom wiped my face and arms with a damp cloth and dried me with a Turkish towel, we sat down at the table. Aunt Rose brought out the pudding in shallow bowls, still warm and creamy. She sprinkled it with a little cinnamon. And we ate.

"You want to go see the horses today, Joey?" Aunt Rose asked, trying to perk me up. It was the last thing I wanted. I finished my Cream, and all I wanted was for Mom to give me a bath and put me to bed. But I didn't even mention that, afraid she'd wrangle the truth out of me.

"It's the stable where the mounted police keep their horses," Rosemarie said. Aunt Rose had been taking Rosemarie and her brother Anthony there for years.

I learned that "the horses" was a code for an old wives' tale the Italian side of the family brought with them from Basilicata, because Aunt Rose and the other sisters—Mary, Millie, my mother, and Aunt Marge—all believed that kids our age should inhale the smell of horse dung to make us strong, healthy and able to withstand the trials of housing project life. And the stink of factories under the bridge.

Before the Cisco-Pancho fiasco, I always wanted to go. But today? Not at all.

WHEN WE WALKED toward the stable, I could see the Silvercup Bakery on the corner. From how I reacted, Aunt Rose must have gathered that the Silvercup brought up worse memories for me than just having gotten lost. So, she walked us in the opposite direction, underneath the bridge toward the East River. Laura looked at me and mouthed something I couldn't understand. By the look on her face, she must have been saying "Eddie" because she pointed at her shoes, until Aunt Rose looked at her in a funny way—forcing Laura to shut up.

The horse stable was an old, whitewashed wooden building that looked ancient and out of place in a neighborhood of brick warehouses blackened by soot and smoke from all the factories in the area, not to mention exhaust from cars entering and exiting the bridge.

It was a steamy summer afternoon. When we arrived at the stable, we heard the horses neighing, and saw their hooves stomping beneath the doors of their stalls. The minute we stepped inside, our lungs almost exploded from the rank smell of horse dung rising off the stable floors. This was why we were there? Rosemarie and I turned to one another with wretched prune faces. We grabbed our noses. We almost lost Aunt Rose's good Cream.

As we slowly started to get our stomachs back, we saw police officers tending their horses. We were skittering around, throwing straw at each other, inhaling the wretched smells—trying to imagine it being good for us—when one officer said to another: "We found the guy at the bottom of the East River."

"Cement buckets?" his partner said.

"Yeah, it's getting to be a habit."

"And the way he was dressed . . . "

"Expensive linen," the other one said. "Looked like a Florida dandy."

"How 'bout those shoes?"

They both laughed. "They didn't wanna mess 'em up with concrete, so they strung the laces together and tied 'em around the poor bastard's neck."

Rosemarie and I were clutching one another behind one of the stalls. We were inhaling deeply now. Not because we wanted to strengthen our lungs. We were terrified. I started to feel asphyxiated again, like when I was trampled under that rushing torrent of kids. I couldn't breathe. I felt like I was drowning. It all sounded so familiar. A few days earlier, we'd heard about expensive linen suits from Miami while we ate pasta fagioli—I mean pasta fazool—in the back of Dad's shoe shop. As we inhaled deeper and deeper, trying to stay quiet and not panic, we both started to get queasy. Aunt Rose noticed our faces and ushered us quickly out of the stables, not so much to protect us from talk of bodies and drownings as to avoid subjecting herself to another look at her precious Cream.

Maybe "going to see the horses" to make our lungs strong wasn't that healthy for kids in Long Island City after all.

Replicating the father's bad habits

CAN A CHILD'S SELF-MEDICATION, *fevers, and encounters with devouring machinery be a subconscious means of reenacting his father's misfortunes and bad habits? The wringer washing machine incident—a reenactment of entrapment?*

My trampling at the Silvercup—subconsciously reliving my father's being pushed down and smothered by his shady deals and complications with money? Were they my own invented means of hiding from it all? My own reenactments of his tragic deeds?

The cowgirl fantasy I used as a coping mechanism to hide from the chaos of my early life? Influenced and plagued by the unhealthy actions I saw before my eyes. Repeating similar actions ad nauseum, then creating more soothing images (telling stories) to "lick the wounds?"

As children, we repeat the bad actions over and over and easily begin to accept them as our own.

Chapter Nine:
Mom Makes *Pasta e Lenticchie*
but Dad Wants *Arroz con Pollo*

A LOT OF OLD-TIME ITALIANS in our neighborhood used to joke about lentils being the beefsteak of Basilicata, the region in Italy that Mom's side of the family had emigrated from. The region was so poor, they said, that every mother learned to cook a variety of vegetables and legumes in such flavorful ways that no one ever noticed not having meat.

Mom always started her pasta lenticchie (Mom pronounced it "lendique") with a mixture of chopped celery, onion, and carrots, sautéed in olive oil until it was dark, aromatic, and flavorful. It was how her mother had made it. Whenever she tried to start it with a ham hock from the butcher, or with a few strips of bacon the way some other Italian mothers had taught her, everyone in the family would tell her it was wrong.

In fact, Mom couldn't make any modern adjustments to any dish she cooked for us because someone would always notice and complain.

"No, don't put the flavoring in first," Dad said when he and I had come back from the shoe shop and Mom was stirring up the gravy.

"This is how I always do it, Herman," she said. "What's the difference anyway? It all goes down the same pipe."

"What's the difference?" Dad said, "I'll tell ya da difference. When you put the flava in first it disappears. Lentils is a taste all its own. You put the flava in later. Trust me."

"Trust you?" Ma said. "You know what you can do, Herman?"

"Yeah, yeah, I know," Dad said.

Mom told him anyway: *"O mangi questa minestra, o salti dalla fenestra."*

"I know," Dad said. "You told me a million times, 'Either eat this soup or throw yourself out the window.' But we got bars on the window, so I might throw the soup out instead."

Mom bit her finger at him and went back into the kitchen.

After they both calmed down, Dad settled into a chair at the dining room table just outside the kitchen door so he could talk to Mom while she cooked. He grabbed together his animal comforts: the sports page, a pack of Camels, an ashtray, and a bottle of Rheingold.

"Anna Pacinello says she puts her macaroni right inta the soup raw and lets it cook," Mom said. "She told me that way the macaroni picks up the flavor of the lentils."

"Don't go trying nothin', Nonny," Dad said, lighting up a cigarette. "It's perfect the way you make it."

"Then why you telling me to start it with bacon?"

"I know something about cookin' too," Dad said. "Besides, I like to get my ideas across."

"Yeah, Herman, if you know something about cooking, how come I never seen you lift a pot?"

Dad growled.

"Herman, I get tired of doin' it the same way all the time."

"Hey, I get tired, too," Dad said. "When was the last time you made arroz con pollo?"

"Not this again." Mom pursed her lips and tried to ignore him.

"Don't you have a half a chicken left over in da fridge?"

Mom smirked and nodded her head.

"Pull that out, wouldja? I'll tell ya how to make arroz con pollo. It'll go great with da lentils."

"I know your recipe, Herman," she said. "YOU told ME a million times! Please shut up. I'll do it. As long as you don't tell me."

Dad started to recite the recipe and Mom started to whine. But she knew it was no use fighting him once he had something on his mind.

So, he went through the whole description while sitting there, his bare feet curled up underneath his buttocks on the chair, smoking a cigarette, and defiantly dropping ashes over Mom's clean dining room floor. Here's what he told her and, dutifully, here's what she did. Maybe if only to shut him up.

She took a day-old cooked chicken out of the fridge, picked the meat off the bones, chopped it into one-inch cubes, and placed them on a sheet pan and warmed them in the oven.

For the Spanish rice, she took 3 to 4 cups of cold leftover rice (yes, once again out of the fridge, because the fridge was Mom's larder), and made a mixture of diced celery, carrots, and onions sautéed in a little olive oil. She added a tablespoon of tomato paste mixed in with a little water. She splashed in a few more tablespoons of olive oil, poured the rice into the pan and turned up the heat for a few minutes, frying it to make it crispy. Now she could place the rice on individual plates and top it with the warmed chicken. And maybe Dad would be happy.

When Dad finished reciting the recipe to Mom, he got lost in the sports page. After scanning the ball scores and thumbing the women's underwear ads, he noticed an item at the back of the sports page. His olive complexion turned pasty. He read out loud:

"Eddie Ryan, a small-time Irish loan shark, entrepreneur, and resident of Long Island City, was found at the bottom of the

East River yesterday. His feet had been encased in buckets filled with . . ."

"Herman," Ma insisted. "Stop right there. We don't want to hear this nonsense."

So, Dad avoided the bad stuff and went on. ". . . suggesting some sort of gangland revenge."

"HERMAN!!!"

No use. Still reading: ". . . Eddie was known affectionately to his friends as Grimy Eddie and is survived by his wife, Estelle."

I guess a young kid's memory is etched by those experiences linked together, because I can't even think about arroz con pollo without calling up the happy-go-lucky face of Eddie Ryan, when we last saw him in his linen suit.

DAD DROPPED THE NEWSPAPER and walked into the living room. Mom had only heard part of it, but the part she did hear, about cement buckets and "gangland" revenge, must have gotten to her.

"Herman," she said, walking out of the kitchen with a spoonful of rice in her hand. "I wish you wouldn't read those kinda things around Joey."

Dad looked over at me and Laura and mumbled, "I thought Freddie said he'd give Eddie a broken arm."

"HERMAN!" Ma said,

Dad said nothing.

He stared out the window, smoking his cigarette, hugging himself around his shoulders as if he had chills. When Mom finally got Dad to budge, we sat down to a plate of arroz con pollo with pasta e lenticchie. To serve it Mom placed a big mound of cooked fried rice on a plate and then put the crispy pieces of chicken on top. Next to the rice she ladled a big helping of the lentils. It tasted good, but felt a little odd, for more reasons than the strange combination. It was my first Italia-Rican meal.

Dad was quiet for a few days. He wasn't cracking any jokes. He wasn't singing "Oh, say can you see any bedbugs on me" like he always did. Even when a pretty lady walked by, he wouldn't nudge me with his elbow and make that clicking sound out of the side of his mouth. Even though Dad had been pretty quiet about the whole mess, he reminded Laura and me that, from now on, we didn't call Federico "Freddie," nor refer to his mother's soup as pasta fagioli; instead, it was "Federico" and "pasta fazool." And we listened.

After a week or so, he came back to life, but he didn't mention a word about Eddie. Not to anyone.

One day after school, Dad and I were in the shoe shop; Dad was out front, while I was in back cutting out pieces of leather. Freddie the bookie came in. "Federico," I mean.

"Herman, goomba. How's d' shoes y' promised me?"

"Dey're ready," Dad said. "I put the new heels on and gave 'em another spit shine. And dey're ready ta go."

"But Herman," Federico said. "You're sure this guy won't be back to pick up his shoes?"

"Trust me," Dad said. "This guy's never comin' back."

That was all Federico needed to hear. There was a code that no explanations were necessary in certain circumstances. This was one of them. As long as Federico didn't ask, Herman didn't say a word. He also didn't ask Freddie about Eddie, the broken arm, the revenge. He didn't want to know.

"How much is it gonna cost me, Herman?"

"Fagetaboutit," Dad said. "I'm doing it for nuthin'."

"Herman, no."

"I already made so much dough on doze shoes," Dad said, "It's criminal . . ." But the minute the word came out of his mouth, Dad backpedaled. "I mean, Federico, everything you've done for me . . ."

"No, Herman, I can't," Federico said. "How about if I put ten dollars down as a bet for you. Tomorrow's the big game."

He was talking about the one-game playoff for the National League Pennant between the Giants and the Dodgers. Everyone was eager to watch the game because no one on this side of the East River cared about the Yankees; they were either a Giants fan or a Dodgers fan.

"There's a lot of money riding on this one, Herman."

"Okay Freddie, whatever you say."

"So, ten on the Dodgers?"

"No, I'm going with New York, not Brooklyn," Dad said.

"Herman?"

"I got a hunch about dis one," Dad said.

"But Herman, the Dodgers are your team. You must've lost 500 bucks in the past couple years."

"I know," Dad said. "Dey're bums. Put da twenty on da Giants."

"Ten, Herman!"

"Oh, sure Freddie, but I thought maybe, since . . ."

"Shut up, Herman. It's ten."

"Sure Freddie, sure."

"Okay, Herman," Freddie said. "But ya know you get in trouble bettin' against your own team. It's like betting against ya family. Sicilians don't like that. I don't know how you Puerto Ricans are."

"Don't axe me ta 'splain it," Dad said.

So, for once, Dad had the last word.

By the time we realize what's happening, it's too late:

AS A TEENAGER I HAD AN INKLING *that it was too late to change who I had become.*

Were Dad's unseemly actions, his lying, his "robbing Peter to pay Paul," behind my acting up, telling stories, using fantasy to cope? I certainly couldn't have understood such things back then.

Even in adulthood, the early experiences that had formed me made me fear I was already who I would be for the rest of my life.

Years into midlife my wife, Gayle, would say, "All those people are dead now. They can't hurt you." But by then it was the emotions that lingered and still hurt. It was too late. I had already become my father—by emulation, by mimicking, by shadowing and mirroring his many bad habits.

Is it possible to escape these inherited habits, to steer them in a more positive direction? On occasion, I feel a calm acceptance: a realization that may never completely cure my transgressions, or mean-spirited behavior, nor give me permanent salvation. Yet these new insights have given me a subtle sense of relief.

Chapter Ten:
Cooked Water and a Sicilian Omen

AFTER DAD SAID, "YOU BACK THERE, JOEY?" I crept out from behind the curtain with my leather cuttings and my scissors in hand.

"We got a big bet going," Dad said, with some bravado. "But don't tell ya mutha." Why was he telling me if he didn't want me to squeal?

"Ya father's a pretty fart smella, Joey," Dad joked. But he was serious, too. He always told his friends that I was a "pretty fart smella."

"But a smart man doesn't bet with his heart," he'd say. "I want the Dodgers so bad, but if I bet for them, I know they'll lose. It's no sweat off me because I refused the ten dollas Freddie offered me for the heels. I have my pride. But if we win, we got most of the money for the doctor."

Since Dad seemed to be talking to himself, I just kept on cutting my leather pieces.

"Joey, I swear, it's an intellectual insight from outta nowhere." The word "intellectual" might not seem like Dad. But it was. "In-te-lec-tu-al." It clicked off Dad's tongue just like all the other fancy words he used.

That afternoon Mom made aquacotta.

"Cooked Water?" It didn't make sense. Except that water played a big part in our lives. Everywhere I turned, water haunted me.

Water, Dad said, was the magic ingredient in fixing the scar on Eddie's shoes. It certainly was what led to his end. Whenever I thought about how Eddie had disappeared, it suffocated me. I had nightmares about the torrential river of kids at the Silvercup Bakery. I felt like I was drowning; I'd wake up sweating, unable to breathe.

Water surrounded me. The night Dad breathed life into me was the same night Dr. Boccardi prescribed aglio e olio instead of aspirin. Mom said that to make the creamy sauce you had to finish the pasta off with a ladle of water. The aquacotta fit right in, water being the main ingredient. Early in the day, Mom fried up some onions and mushrooms in olive oil until they were dark brown. Then she put the leftover onion skins, some mushroom stems, and zucchini trimmings in another pot and covered them with the water. She cooked it down until she had a rich vegetable broth. Then she strained the broth and poured it into the sauté mixture along with some tomatoes, herbs, salt, and pepper. This was a thick, dark soup, as shady as one of Dad's deals. As murky as the East River current where Eddie was last seen.

Mom also made verdura, or broccolini in lemon and garlic sauce. She poached some broccolini until it was tender. Then she made a separate mixture of lemon juice, olive oil, chopped parsley, and minced garlic. Later she would pour the lemon juice mixture over the greens just before serving.

Mom had made up some chicken cutlets that afternoon, too. She put the boned chicken breasts between two pieces of wax paper and pounded them thin, then coated them, first with flour, then with beaten egg, then with seasoned breadcrumbs. She fried them in a little oil until they were golden brown.

As was Mom's habit, she made the entire meal early so she

could sit down and enjoy it with us. This also allowed everything to come to room temperature so all the flavors could meld.

Later that day the playoff game between the Bums and the Giants came on the radio. Everywhere you went, people were glued to the play-by-play broadcast by Mel Allen, the voice that made baseball come to life. Dad was sweating, pacing around the shop, chain-smoking cigarettes, and throwing empty cigarette packages everywhere. Things looked bad for Dad because the Dodgers seemed to have the game won. I was only guessing he had bet on the Giants because of what he had told me earlier that morning. Finally, in the bottom of the ninth, Bobby Thompson came to bat. And when he hit the home run, Mel Allen went wild and so did Dad.

Instead of pacing, now Dad was running in circles, his head and hands gesturing toward heaven. "Twenty bucks," he yelled at the top of his lungs. "Twenty Bucks!"

The Giants had won the game in their last at-bat and Dad had won the bet. The people who were in the shop at the time couldn't believe Dad's reaction to his beloved Dodgers losing. They knew he hated the Giants. But they also knew he was unpredictable.

When we sat down to dinner later that night, Dad said "Everything's peachy, Nonnie. I got the money fa Joey's doctor bill."

"Where'd it come from?"

But Dad ignored her. "What's fa dinner?" he asked.

"Aquacotta," I said proudly.

"Ah, cooked water," Dad said with that snarl of his. "Whenever I think of cooked water I always think of Eddie—that dirty little Irishman, decked out in his linen suit—going down in style."

"HERMAN!!"

"What, Nonny? Eddie was in the wrong place at the wrong time."

"I don't care about Eddie. I want to know how you got the money for the doctor bill."

"So what else is fa dinner?" Dad said.

"Herman?"

"Aquacotta's not a meal, Nonny."

"We got cutlets and verdura," Mom said. "It didn't cost much. Who knows when we'll see the money for the doctor bill."

"Ma," I chimed in. "Today, Dad . . . " But I stopped short. I remembered what Dad had said earlier, when he put his hand down on his belt and told me to keep my mouth shut.

Dad just stared at me. So I kept silent. He reached over for some stale bread and broke it up into his bowl. I remembered what I'd overheard Dad talking to Freddie about: the money was from gambling. And Mom was already starting to boil over because she knew about the playoff game. But maybe she just let it go because she knew the bill would finally get paid.

The loud knock at the door would change all that.

THE DOOR WAS FLUNG OPEN and Laura and I looked at one another in fear, wondering who would burst in like that, remembering that Cousin Gloria often showed up at dinnertime, stealing bites of food off our plate. But it was Uncle Johnny, so Laura leaned toward me and whispered: "Uncle doesn't like aquacotta or verdura. And he'd rather eat pork rinds than cutlets. So, don't worry—our food is safe."

Mom got up to greet him and they talked for a minute. Or, I mean Uncle Johnny did: *Hello, Annie . . . I already ate . . . Just gotta talk ta my brotha . . . Herman home?*

"Hey, Johnny," Dad said.

Johnny came to the table and practically dragged Dad back into the bedroom. Mom had seen it before, so she smirked and watched them go.

"Ya fatha's got more deals going than Carter has little pills," she muttered, shaking her dishtowel at him. "When's he gonna learn?"

There were some loud moans from the bedroom at first; but then long moments of silence. They both came out quietly. Johnny passed the table, nodded to Mom, and left. Dad sat down to eat his aquacotta as if nothing had happened.

"Herman?" Mom said.

"Yeah, Nonny?"

"What's going on?"

"Nothing."

"HERMAN," she said louder. "What happened?"

Dad just stared into the bowl of cooked water in front of him.

"It's da deal I was tellin' ya about," he said. "The money just got lost in transit."

As Laura would tell me later, "transit" was another one of those words that was supposed to make him sound in control.

You could tell by the look on Mom's face she didn't have enough energy to keep nagging my father about his wheeling and dealing. She shook her head and sighed.

The meal got awfully quiet. We all put some chunks of stale bread into our bowls. Then Mom ladled the broth on top. In my mind, I saw Eddie being covered over by the East River, the broth dark and foreboding.

When the verdura and cutlets came, we finished them off. Then they sent me to bed where I could dream about the cowgirls.

THE NEXT DAY LAURA TOLD ME what she knew about Freddie and the shoes—from a night she had been with Rosemarie and Uncle Johnny, when I'd gone to mass with Mom and Aunt Rose, and Dad was "off galivanting somewhere," as Mom would often say.

Freddie used to haunt the same bar in Coney Island where

Dad and Johnny had been spouting off about Dad's handi-work with the cordovan French-toes. On the night Laura told me about, Rosemarie, Uncle, and Laura were in Sal's Bar when Freddie stopped in on his way back from Staten Island to get one for the road. Freddie said he was celebratin', Laura told me.

When Sal asked, "What's the occasion?" Freddie said, "These shoes I got from Herman to settle his vig." (The vig was what some other gamblers called "liquorish," a tiny bit of interest every loan shark or bookie charged for loaning money or taking a bet.)

Sal fell silent. He looked terrified, Laura told me. Before he could say anything, Johnny started waving to Sal behind Fred-die's back, signaling him to shut up. But it was too late.

"Those were Eddie's shoes," Sal said. "He bought 'em in Boca but they got a scar across the toe, so Herman . . ."

"Hey, Goomba," Johnny shouted.

Freddie's voice started to rumble. It started low and ended up an animalistic groan. He stalked over to the pool table, picked up a pool cue and broke it over his knee.

Sal calmed Freddie down by forcing him to knock back a shot of Four Roses. Perched on a barstool, Freddie started to take the shoes off the minute he began to control his rage. But then he stopped. Federi-co had his pride, and he wasn't about to traipse home to

Queens on eight changes of subway line in his stocking feet. Besides, Freddie knew that the damage had already been done.

Laura explained it to me years later: for a Sicilian to be walking around in a dead man's shoes was a bad omen.

According to Laura, Freddie got on the train with fiery rage, a scowl on his face, and the cordovan French-toes still on his feet.

When Uncle Johnny had told the story to Dad in the bedroom the night before, while we ate our aquacotta, Dad must have realized he was already floating in some pretty hot water himself.

Johnny, Rose, and Laura headed back to the Queensborough Plaza on the same train as Freddie, but they knew they'd better keep a distance, so they rode the next car, still able to see Freddie within their view, dealing with his predicament.

Johnny told my father that, sure, Freddie got on the train in Coney, still wearing the shoes. But on his second change of trains, he ran into a couple of hoods from Brooklyn. Whether they were Sicilian brothers or Neapolitans just trying to get the best of him, they convinced Freddie that the longer he wore those shoes, the worse the omen would get; in fact, the omen would turn into a curse. I'm sure, this is all b.s., but sworn to be true, in third-hand stories handed down from Uncle to cousin to sister to me. And maybe it contributed to the myth of why my father's screwed-up life was so convoluted.

Well, Freddie took off the shoes right on the subway train as it rattled its way toward Queensborough Station. Freddie sat staring out the window as the local stations passed by. He was alone in his world of embarrassment—until people started staring at him. So he got up and stalked from car to car, accosting people, forcing them to rummage through their packages for an extra bag in which to carry the shoes.

Finally, blinded by his anger, he found himself standing in front of an old bum who was sleeping across two seats. The bum woke up to the sight of Freddie's stockinged feet. Freddie felt something wet. When he looked down he understood why: he was standing in a puddle of beer. Freddie was too pissed off to move, but he followed the trail of beer to a bottle the bum had spilled. Freddie lifted the bottle out of the bag, only to see that it was Rheingold, my father's favorite brand, another part of the so-called Sicilian omen. I could only imagine Rose, Uncle, and my sister standing at one of the closed train doors, all three leaning over to stare through the window into what was going on with Freddie in the next compartment, because I'd seen many people doing it when some strange, dramatic event took place on an adjacent subway car. It happened all the time.

Freddie began shaking, Laura said. His animal growl began to drown out the rumble of the subway, his feet sopping wet. He just stood there looking at his feet and then at the shoes, which he held, dangling from his index and middle fingers. Suddenly, he realized he had no choice but to use the brown paper bag—soggy with the stench of beer—to put the shoes in so he could carry them home, and to hide at least that reminder of his embarrassment. His sopping stocking feet made wet footprints on the train floor wherever he walked, there for all the world—at least the underground world that rides the BMT at 3 o'clock on a Sunday morning—to see.

And someone was going to have to pay: that someone was Herman Emelio Ortiz. My Dad. "The pretty fart smella." The genius. According to my Uncle Johnny, "The best goddamn shoe repairman in the greater New York area."

Convoluted, terrifying stories . . .
that turn humorous

I WANTED THE MUSICAL TO BE FUNNIER *than it turned out. Perhaps my memory caused me to color the pain with the humor that always seemed to be a part of our coping strategy.*

Little did I realize that terrifying stories often turned humorous as a peasant device to divert angst and suffering. So, all the chaos—the crazy nights of shouting; neighbors storming into the house scream-ing about a fight down on the block; relatives in a revolving turnstile through the living room and kitchen, swearing that their way to fry a veal cutlet was the only acceptable technique—often were turned into humorous stories when they were retold. They became the salve that made my story easier to digest and the courage to look at the underlying painful experiences. If I'd known that the memoirist journey would ultimately be one of terrifying self-discovery, I might never have been willing to embark.

Cousin Johnny, who got left out of this account because putting him in would have made the book 600 pages long, could tell a harrowing anecdote and make you bust your gut with laughter. He must have learned the peasant trick of turning lemons into lemon-ade. And he knew how to lie to tell a fascinating story. I suppose I learned how to write fiction from him, too.

The World Premiere
of
Joe Ortiz's
Musical Memoir

Jon Nordgren, Producing Artistic Director

Poster for the Musical at Cabrillo Stage (design by Jana Marcus).

Chapter Eleven:
The Kitchen Window

THE QUEENSBOROUGH PROJECTS is a series of buildings that look like winding canyon walls made from bricks of a blood-red color. Dark blood. The areas between the zigzag buildings—paths, burnt-out lawn areas, and playgrounds—felt like a big cauldron in which all the local aromas, emotions, and information swirled together in a teeming ethnic stew.

The aroma of matzoh-ball soup would filter down from the Glicklicks' apartment, and you'd hear Yiddish-accented discussions about a sale on overcoats at the local haberdashery; Irish stew wafted from the building across the way, and along with it, a story about a brawl at the local tavern; the smell of Cuban rice and beans was accompanied by a naming of Salsa bands in from Havana that would headline at the Palladium that weekend; the scent of gravy, onions, and stewed tomatoes floated in the air along with a description of Jackie Robinson stealing home.

The kitchen window was our connection to the world. Whatever you wanted to know, you learned it there. When opened wide enough, it transformed the projects into one big living room. For example, the moment Mrs. Vynella heated olive oil in a skillet and threw in a handful of chopped garlic, Mom could not only hear it but smell the aroma, too. She knew Mrs. Vynella was starting her sautéed verdura. "Yoo hoo, Angie," Mom would yell out the window, leaning out and looking up. "I don't have enough garlic.

"Could I come up for a clove?"

We kids just threw things up and down to one another between floors using only our hands, while the adults used a colander or a basket. When it was something precious or essential, like garlic or a cup of sugar, the mothers always walked up or down the stairs to get it. They didn't have the same faith in throwing or catching that we kids had, or that they themselves had in, say, the Immaculate Conception. Of course, by yelling out the window Mom could find out if Mrs. Vynella had what she needed in the first place. Garlic is a bad example, though. Any Italian mother caught without garlic in the kitchen at any given moment was looked on as if she didn't have a calendar in the house on New Year's Day, or a set of rosary beads close to the crucifix.

For many inhabitants their only link to the outside world was their kitchen windows. Mrs. DeAngelo, from the building across from us, conducted her whole life from a yellow Formica table in her kitchen, where she knitted, smoked Chesterfields, and drank coffee all day long. As Uncle Frank once said on a rare visit from Brooklyn, "Mrs. DeAngelo's got her ass glued to that chair. If she's gone from da table, I guarantee ya, she's eeda sittin' onna terlet or she got up ta stir da gravy."

If you needed to know anything, Mrs. DeAngelo knew the details. She could spot Aunt Rose walking up from the bus stop, Dad coming home from work, Dr. Boccardi on his way for a house call.

And she'd let you know about it.

Bill collectors or bookies were hard for Mrs. DeAngelo to figure. If she couldn't identify someone, she was quiet for a while; she knew not to talk too soon and tip them off. She'd warn you when they were at the corner, point to them silently as they approached, and, after they went into the building, she'd say something in code, like, ". . . the chicken just went into the oven." Mrs. DeAngelo's warnings were how the whole world knew our business.

Mrs. DeAngelo said her lumbago prevented her from going out. For me it was the iron bars on the kitchen window that prevented me from falling. My parents installed them just for that purpose, knowing I wanted to be part of the action.

Mom's constant phrase—the one she used when we complained about her cooking, "O, ti mangia questa minestra, o salti dalla fenestra"— had a sort of peasant irony. How could you send soup out the window? Just throw it through the bars, I suppose.

As with everything else we discovered, it was through the kitchen window that Mom slowly learned how deep of a jam Dad was in.

"D'ya hear about Eddie Ryan, Annie?" Mrs. Vynella said. "I heard that Herman was fixing his shoes."

"Ya tryin' ta say Herman was mixed up in this?" Mom said, indignantly. She waited for Angie's response but got nothing.

So, Mom finally broke the silence:

"Yeah, I heard," Mom said. "They say he drowned. But I don't know nothin' about no shoes."

Like the aromas from all the diverse ethnic foods floating up to our apartment, Mom always saw Dad's situation in a murky, soupy sort of way. She always treated Dad's schemes as creating an embarrassment, maybe the loss of a little money, but nothing too serious or life threatening—nothing that hadn't happened before and couldn't be cured by scrimping and saving and eating rice and beans for a few weeks.

Now Mom could keep herself in the dark no longer. Dad

might have seemed safe at the moment. But if Mom found out the whole story, it might plunge Dad in a lot of hot and crazy water: acquapazza, I guess. This situation was worse than that. The water for Mom's pasta was boiling away. She needed garlic. Still, she wanted to know about the shoes. Laura sensed what was going on so she tried to sneak out by making believe she had to sing with the doo-wop guys down on the block. But Mom cornered her. She grabbed her by the ear and twisted until Laura began to spill the beans.

Just then Mrs. Vynella yelled up, "Yoo hoo, I got the garlic for you. Come up."

Sometimes Laura talked so fast she got confused. In that moment, she blurted out Freddie's name. Fortunately, Mom was distracted about getting dinner on the table. So she let go of Laura's ear and told her she wanted "some answers, Miss Prim, as soon as I'm back from getting the garlic."

On "Going Away"

DISTRACTION BECAME A SAFE PLACE. *A way to quell the maddening chaos of reality.*

I could distract myself with an image, or a game, or an object just within reach—food, music, storytelling, perhaps a fantasy: the images of cowboys, the cowgirls taking flight in my imagination riding across the bedroom walls, the designs and colors in my mother's drapery and fabrics.

Escapes into multi-textured patterns became my salvation. A tangible surface to concentrate on when the going got tough, the chaos too intense—when the yelling in the room overpowered me or the coming and going of neighbors and relatives, combined with dramatic situations, became too nerve-wracking to endure.

These self-devised focal points of imposed bliss must be where art is born, the refuge of damaged little boys and girls. Pain disguised in fiction; fabricated mental constructions to replace reality.

In the midst of that self-saving creative process, being lost in fantasies suddenly became being found.

These were the moments I found myself "going away," only to hear someone say, "Are you in there, Joey? Come back."

Dad on Thanksgiving singing "Begin the Beguine." We replicated his insanity in the musical, with Adam Saucedo doing a rendition of two original songs written just for the show.

110

Chapter Twelve:
Pastina: Food for the Soul

DAD HAD OFTEN SEEN me poking my head through the security bars on our kitchen window, so one night he started mimicking me for a change, laying it on real thick so I would believe he was really stuck.

"Help me," he clowned in his whiney Puerto Rican voice, flapping his arms and squealing like a chicken. "Joey, help me. I can't get out! My head's stuck inna bars."

"Let me try, Daddy," I said. "Let me try." For better or worse, my father was my hero and I wanted to do whatever he did.

But as usual, Dad didn't stick around to watch. He just headed for the door and left to buy his beer for dinner. Mom was still gone fetching garlic downstairs and Laura was in the living room listening to her Patti Page records on the Victrola. So, I went up to the window and stuck my head through the bars.

In the ten minutes of pretending my head was stuck, people began leaning out of their kitchen windows—a ladle or a spatula in one hand and a tumbler of red wine in the other—taking a break from stirring the gravy on their stoves.

Just then Mrs. DeAngelo, sitting at her kitchen window in the apartment building across from ours, said she spotted somebody walking up from Twenty-First Street.

"Federico Patriarca's coming," she said. "He's looking for somebody."

I craned my neck and could see Freddie walking up. He had that same indignant look on his face that he had when you said "fagioli" instead of "fazool." I yelled over my shoulder to Laura, who was still flipping through records at the Victrola.

"Joey, stop joking," she said.

"I'm not joking. It's Freddie comin' up the walk."

The intoxicating scent of sausages, peppers, tomatoes, garlic, and olive oil coming from every kitchen window in the Queensborough Projects distracted me from thinking about Freddie for a moment; and overpowered the aroma of Mom's gravy: Lasagna bolognese with red meat sauce—that unmistakable aroma with just a hint of cinnamon and cloves; meatballs made with grated Parmesan cheese, eggs, parsley, and onions, simmering in a frying pan until they were dark and succulent. I smelled garlic fried in olive oil, the first step in hundreds of dishes; pasta e fagioli, the soup of beans and macaroni—made a thousand ways—that caused heated arguments between Dad and Freddie.

Yeah, Freddie! Now making his way up the pathway to our building that very moment.

JUST THEN DAD WALKED IN the door. He must have snuck in from what we kids called "going over the roof"—a shortcut Laura and her friends used when playing Cowboys and Indians; but she never told Mom or she would have caught hell. Having never been up there myself, I had only a murky idea of the route; but just thinking about it brought even more anguish to my chest: I imagined them all walking on a tight-rope wire or out on a ledge.

As I learned later, you could go up the stairwell of our apartment, through a door that opened onto a contiguous roof that connected our building to the building behind ours. That building's stairwell led down to other apartments, eventually letting you out an entry to the street right under Queensborough Bridge. Laura, Rosemarie, and their friends used to call it "the Tar Beach," for obvious reasons: on blisteringly hot summer days, kids and parents alike would go up to the roof to get some sun, Coney being forty minutes and eight subway changes away; they'd come back down to their apartments complaining that their beach chairs and sandals got stuck in the melting roof tar. But Dad had his own routine: he often went up to the roof to drink beer or smoke. Sometimes he'd cross over the roof in order to avoid the bill collector or anyone else he didn't want to face.

When Dad saw me with my head caught, he wasn't fooled.

"Stop jokin' around, Joey," he said. "Ya trying to make believe ya head's stuck inna bars?"

"No, Dad, Freddie's comin'."

"Stop jokin' wit me," Dad said, raising his voice.

Then, when we heard Mrs. DeAngelo yelling, "Yoo hoo, Herman. Freddie's walking up the walkway to your building," Dad panicked. He believed her!

Before anything else could happen—before Dad could put his beer in the fridge, check the gravy, or even help me out of the bars, Mrs. DeAngelo offered her coded warning: "The chicken just got put into the soup kettle. Make sure it doesn't boil over." And just then, the door slammed and Dad disappeared again. Had he gone back over the roof to avoid Freddie coming up the stairs?

I tried to pull my head out of the bars, but now my head really was stuck. I didn't have the strength to spread the bars apart and escape like Dad. I couldn't budge. Other agonies popped into my mind: the ringer washing machine; the trampling at the bakery; Eddie being found in the East River. I didn't want to think about being trapped, so, standing there with my head stuck between wrought-iron bars, I escaped into fantasies of cowgirls and my mother's good pasta.

113

It seemed like an eternity since Mom had gone down to Mrs. Vynella's for a clove of garlic. I could hear Laura in the living room humming along with the radio to "How Much is That Doggie in the Window." I thought they were singing about me. But I wasn't about to say anything. I didn't want to get in trouble.

Finally—as quickly as I had discovered I was stuck—my neck had rolled over to a new position and my head slid out. I was free.

When Mama got back from fetching the garlic, she went right back to cutting up a chicken to make broth for pastina. She put the chicken in eight cups of boiling water along with a carrot, a stalk of celery, and a roughly chopped onion.

She had no idea I had even been trapped.

FREDDIE BURST IN THROUGH THE DOOR, rummaged through the apartment and asked Laura about Dad. I started to cry. I wasn't sure if it was from my fear of Freddie or from all my physical pains. My neck was still tweaked from the bars. I still felt the bruises from the Silvercup bakery incident and the washing machine. Mrs. Vynella had always said, "It's a good thing a young kid's bones can bend." But what about Dad? His bones would probably just snap. Freddie lit up a cigarette. He stood there leaning against the kitchen entryway. When he started adjusting something bulky under his coat, I began to cry even louder.

Laura said, "Dad's not afraid of you."

"Shut up, kid," Freddie said. He said it slowly while looking away, as if to say, I'm gonna getcha Dad, kids. He doesn't mess with Federico Patriarca.

Freddie made is way toward the door, then turned to Mom and said, "I'll be back." Mom and Laura just stood there, silent, so Freddie stormed out.

A few moments later, Dad came back in and Laura held her

finger up to her mouth, pointing toward the door and mouthing the words "Freddie just left."

Dad tiptoed in and slowly walked toward the bedroom, whispering, "If he comes back, I'm not here."

Dad must have known Freddie might be still waiting down on the landing between floors, because Freddie suddenly rushed back in through the door.

"Herman in, now?" Freddie snapped at Mom.

"No, he just left," my mother covered.

So, Freddie put his hand on the bulge under his coat and said, "He home now?"

"Ahhhhhh, Herman! Get outta here!"

When he heard my mother scream, Dad came running, pulling up his pants and rubbing his eyes as if he'd been resting up just for Freddie's visit.

In the panic Mama let the broth boil over, then quickly— just in time to save it—she rushed over and shut it off. And that turned out to be a slice of good fortune. See, just like everyone on our block, Freddie knew a little something about pastina.

"You shouldn't ova-boil the stock. It'll bruise the broth," Freddie said, sliding his hand away from the bulge under his coat. After you give a man advice about his pastina, it just doesn't seem right to aggravate his wife and family. Believe me, in our neighborhood a man's life often hinged on smaller matters than good soup.

Dad tried to forget about whatever Freddie was hiding under his coat by staring at the simmering broth.

Freddie was right about the stock. Boiling it down helps concentrate the flavor. Cooked down too little, the flavor is weak; too much and the flavor is too intense, the broth too thick. Mom said later she knew what he meant by "bruising it." That was how wise guys talked just about anything. It was a code, their poetic license. Anything could be made to hurt if the situation called for it.

* * * *

FREDDIE GRABBED ONTO DAD'S ARM and walked him into the living room. I played with quarters on the floor under the dining room table. Laura pretended to shuffle records at the Victrola.

Freddie leaned toward Dad. He spoke softly so Mom couldn't hear him.

"Ya know, Herman, last month's vig is not going to disappear," Freddie whispered.

"It's comin' soon, Freddie," Dad said, his lower lip starting to tremble. "Real soon."

Laura and I looked at one another because Dad had told us about the "vig" and what it meant but, as usual, he never finished telling us the rest of the story. When Freddie noticed me and Laura glaring at one another, he said, "Don't lie, Herman."

"I swear it. Would I lie about something this serious? Wit my kids here? I swear . . ."

"OKAY, HERMAN!" But then he calmly grabbed Dad's arm and squeezed.

"Ya know, Herman, I found out about the shoes," Freddie whispered. "I heard the whole story from Sal."

Dad's lower lip started to tremble again. He was silent for a real long time. Laura and I looked up to see what was going on, but Dad just glared at us until we looked away.

"There's a big confusion, Federico," Dad said. "A big, big confusion." There was a long, awkward silence again. Then Dad went on: "Those shoes really weren't the same shoes I fixed fa Eddie."

"Herman," Freddie said. "What would Annie say if you and I had to take a little walk down by the East River?"

"I swear to you, I had to dye Eddie's shoes black ta cover up the cut on the toe. My brotha Johnny was there, he'll tell ya . . ."

That upset Federico a little more. Being reminded that Dad's hiding the cut with ground-up shoe leather and black shoe dye sounded like a cheap Puerto Rican fix. So he worked Dad into a corner, making him squeal in a high-pitched voice by forcing him to agree to a few promises.

"Look, Herman. I ain't covering the bet. You understand?"

Dad became a jabbering idiot. "Sure, Freddie. Sure. Sure. I wouldn't take dat money. Not after this misunderstanding."

"This is not a misunderstanding, Herman."

"I know. I know. I know."

"You owe me big," Freddie said.

"Anything, Federico."

"Remember I told ya I needed a place ta set up book for a few hours? Well, next week I need it."

"Sure Federico, whatever you say," Dad said. "The shoe shop is yours."

Freddie stared at Dad for a long look. "The apartment, Herman."

"Freddie, No, I couldn't. Not here. Annie, the kids . . ."

"Herman?" Federico didn't have to put his hand on his coat. He just said Dad's name and glared at him.

"Okay, pal," Dad said. "No problem. The place is yours."

"And Herman," Freddie said as he started for the door. "I need some proof about the shoes."

"But listen ta me, Freddie . . ."

"No, Herman, No," Freddie said. "Maybe you'd like me to tie those shoes around your neck. Remember what happened to Eddie?"

"But Freddie . . ."

"No, no, no. You're just a fast mouth, Herman. You made me look like a fool—a walking dead man. I need my due. This situation isn't over. I gotta have some proof or I'm not done with you. Either I need to know about the shoes, or I need a piece of you, Herman. The money? Yeah, I need that, too, but I need my due. And it'll come outta your skinny Puerto Rican ass. Nobody knows what really happened to Eddie, Herman. But I know."

Freddie just kept on nodding. He gave Dad a little friendly love-tap across his cheek, walked out and slammed the door behind him.

THERE WAS A LONG, AWKWARD SILENCE after Freddie left. Mom pretended nothing had happened. Laura and I were famished. But by then everything had cooled off a little, including the broth. Mom took the meat off the bone and returned the carcass to the pot for a few more minutes cooking. She placed the shredded chicken on a serving platter and ladled some warm tomato sauce over it for an improvised chicken cacciatore. Then she sautéed up some Swiss chard. And that was dinner. She turned off the broth and we sat down to eat in silence.

Later, after our stomachs and hearts had settled down from dinner and Freddie's visit, Mom looked at the broth and said it was okay. It hadn't burned, it wasn't too thick, it wasn't bruised. She said the word "bruised" with extra emphasis and shot a long, glaring look in Dad's direction. After the broth cooled, Mom put it on a potholder in the refrigerator and we went to bed.

THE NEXT DAY, the whole neighborhood was gabbing about Freddie and my father's gambling and the pistol and the whole mess. My mother just went right on making her pastina. She took the chicken broth out of the fridge and skimmed off the cold, white fat from the top of the pot. She strained the chicken broth with cheesecloth and put it back on the stove to cook down a little more.

After that my mother took off her apron, sat me down on the edge of the table and yelled out to my father in the living room, "Herman, watch Joey and make sure the chicken broth doesn't boil ova. I'll be right back. I gotta get some parsley from Aunt Rose downstairs."

As soon as she was gone, I went to the window and squeezed my head through the bars.

Again! Below me I could see Aunt Rose's hand coming out her window to pick a few springs of parsley from her window box.

That's when I realized my head really was stuck. Again!

Just then I heard my father opening the front door and saying something about needing a pack of smokes. "If the chicken broth starts ta boil, just turn it off," he said. "I'll be right back."

"But Daddy," I squealed, "my head's stuck . . ."

Too late. The door slammed and I was alone. In a minute the broth started to boil. Steam began to crawl down the sides of the kitchen walls and roll out the window above my head.

I started to scream for help but all that did was draw an appreciative crowd, eager for a good laugh. I could hear the broth boiling down, down, down, and I knew my mother was going to be steaming herself when she found out I'd spoiled her hard work. The bars began to tighten around my ears.

Finally, I saw Dad walking up the path below me, carrying his beloved bottle of Rheingold Stout and a carton of Camel straights. He looked cockeyed at the crowd outside our place. Then he spotted me.

"Stop joking around, Joey," he yelled. But then he looked at me again. He could see something in my face and knew I wasn't joking.

He ran up the stairs, put his beer down, checked the pastina, then reached around, grabbed hold of the bars, and spread them like a pair of suspenders. I dropped to the floor like a piece of dirty laundry.

THE CURATIVE EFFECT OF CHICKEN BROTH is something Italians, Jews, and other ethnic groups have long prescribed for any ill fortune, a sort of religious experience tied to suffering and repentance. Even though Aunt Mary used to call soup a "belly wash," she also used to say, "When you sin, you suffer. But to save your soul, all you gotta do is pray. And eat a warm bowl of pastina."

When my mother got done gabbing with Aunt Rose downstairs, she came back up and threw a handful of tiny star macaroni into the broth. Which hadn't been bruised after all. The only thing.

"Don't put too much of the pastina pasta in," she told me. "It grows when it cooks."

All I could think about was my head expanding in the bars.

When the macaroni was cooked, Mom chopped up a few sprigs of the parsley and added it to the soup. We all sat down to a golden, glowing bowl of pastina. With a few sprinkles of black pepper and a little grated parmesan on top, a warm bowl of pastina can lift the weight of any little agony a soul may have to endure.

The Memoir as Recipe:

I'M DEVISING THIS "RECIPE FOR A MEMOIR" to help convince myself that we can reconstruct a story of our past with only the "ingredients we have on hand"—and only those recollections we allow ourselves to remember.

I vividly recall having been eaten alive by Mom's wringer washing machine. I know for sure that it happened. But the events of Dad's tragic downfall with money were mere stories I'd only heard from gossip down on the block and glimpsed through the veil of childhood. Yeah, and even through the lens of my sister's coaxing. So, I did what any kid might do—I invented a connective narrative to explain the inexplicable: how Dad was destined to get himself in such hot water with the neighborhood bookie.

The stories heard around the table—told and retold so often that they became real—were the only clues I had to work with. And, of course, Laura was my translator.

Surely, I must have filtered what I saw and heard. How much of that filter was denial? In an attempt to fashion a story out of a memory I was afraid to recall, I find myself following the path that many writers take in explaining why they write in the first place—to find out what happened. Again, Laura was my eyes and ears.

A memoir—as a recipe, then—might be seen as a way to solve a craving. But, ideally perhaps, it can also be a blueprint for nourishment, for understanding. So, I invent my meal—a main course or a soup—the way one might construct a story. Starting with the raw ingredients.

THE INGREDIENTS:

Narrative (okay, so we're just telling a story)
Scenes in action in a proper order (so they appear to make sense)
Digging up old bones and using condensation
     (to intensify the broth)
Salt and pepper, the seasonings (the spice of occasional imagery)
A sprinkle of fiction (to help hold the reader's attention)

Narrative: We all tell stories. And we carry our recipes around with us, written or in our heads, to create self-nourishment. It's our human nature.

Linking scenes in some logical order: We learn to add ingredients (episodes or scenes) in a specific sequence. And by combining the tragic events that we're absolutely sure happened with those that are hazy or inaccessible, we hope to justify and assuage the painful moments. In building soup from a recipe, for example, we're often compelled to add an extra favorite ingredient to make the preparation our own. (Editors might call these our "darlings" which creep in when we become too lazy to find the proper words.)

Digging up old bones: Old bones, roasted and boiled down in wine or water, add depth and character to the broth. This may call up an image from archaeology—or from self-therapy, where we might peel back a solitary event like an onion. We uncover an old bone from the earth (or our memory) and wonder what secrets it can tell us about our past.

Condensation as Revision: Both cook and writer use condensation by boiling down a stock over low heat (a paragraph into concise language), into its most concentrated essence—to enhance its intensity.

Testing a recipe over and over to perfect it is like revision in writing. We revise to make sure the flavor balance of our dish will please the palate.

Justification and expansion: In reduction, we hope to maintain the balance of the dish (or story), its persuasiveness. But condensation isn't the only technique. Often something has to be added. As any seasoned cook (or writer) will tell you, there are times when new ingredients must be added to the pot, new possibilities explored.

The salt and pepper: After our dish is "almost done," it's advisable to taste it. So, we "correct for seasonings." Thus, a bit more revision is needed. The spice of imagery gives the dish a depth of flavor that makes a soup or a story come to life.

A sprinkling of fiction: Even the relatives sitting around the table, drinking tumblers of red wine, made things up in relating their "personal recipes" of what happened. So, I follow their lead. In the end, we see it all as being true. But as Mom always said, "the proof is in the pudding"—meaning if it rings true (or tastes good) it satisfies our need for nourishment.

From about 2018 to 2024, the creative team of Greg Fritsch, Matt Shelton, and I tossed around the idea of changing the title of the musical to Over the Roof.

Matt, who had offered a concert reading of the play at his theater on Sutter Street in San Francisco, had suggested the idea. Well, it took us those six years of Greg reworking the script to finally make that change. So, we officially make the announcemnt with the publication of Pastina.

Over the Roof -
Escape from Queensbridge

Chapter Thirteen:
Over the Roof

LATER THAT WEEK, Freddie showed up at the apartment as expected. When the bell rang, Mom went to the door with a fake smile on her face—the same exaggerated, sarcastic smile and steely, hateful eyes she flashed at Dad when she had to face his shenanigans. She silently opened the door.

Freddie carried an old, tattered briefcase. He came in, nodded to Mom, and went straight into the living room and right to the telephone. He set up a card table that Dad had left out for him, pulled up a chair and sat down. Out of the briefcase he pulled a disheveled account book and a screwdriver. He turned the phone over and unscrewed the bottom plate. He then pulled out a book of matches and ripped off the cover, folding it over several times, and jammed it into the bell of the telephone.

Later, when someone called, the phone would click instead of ringing. It showed us all that this wise guy who had taken over our house—who was known for maiming, crippling, and even making people vanish—had the decency to muffle the bell on our phone so it wouldn't drive us all crazy.

It was small consolation, though. Just having Freddie in our lives made us uneasy. Even at my young age, I felt put upon and insulted—just as Mom and Laura surely must have been—at this "deal" Dad must have put us through in the name of protecting us, feeding us, and keeping a roof over our heads, but more likely to save his own ass.

The phone clicked away. Each time, after only one or two muffled clicks, Federico picked it up, spoke briefly, jotted down a name and a number in his book, and hung up. This went on for nearly three hours.

When he was all done, he unrigged the phone, put the chair back, folded up the card table, packed up his briefcase, and walked toward the door.

Freddie stopped at the kitchen, glared in at Mama, and said, "Herman and I are even for now. But you know him better than I do. Did he tell you he had some information for me?"

Mom shook her head.

"Herman was supposed to find out about some shoes for me. When you see him just tell him I have to know about the cordovan French-toes."

"Well, he's out paying Joey's doctor bill."

"Well if I see him first the money's mine, and I might take a little chunk out his behind for interest."

He opened the door to leave, then turned to her and said, "And about the shoes. I have to know soon."

I WAS STILL PRETTY SICK at the time. When I wasn't being trampled, gobbled up by machines, or neglected by a drunken father, I suffered from bronchitis. Dr. Boccardi had been trying to convince my mother to get me to a warmer, drier climate. He said, "When he gets older, Annie, he'll develop a strong and athletic chest, but this damp New York weather is going to aggravate his bronchitis." That night, when Dad came home, Mom said, "Herman, Dr. Boccardi says we should take Joey to Arizona or he's going to be a real sick boy fa the rest of his life."

If Mom expected resistance, she didn't show it.

She stood there with her arms folded.

"Nonnie," Dad said. "I been thinking about it and ye'r right." Mom got suspicious.

"My brotha Johnny's going ta California," Dad said. "I neva told ya because I didn't want you to worry." He paused a minute, then laid the bomb: "I'm leaving fa Los Angeles inna mornin'."

"Herman," Mom said. "HERMAN! You're leaving? You've been planning this, and you didn't even tell me?"

"I knew you'd get upset."

"Boccardi said Arizona, Herman. Arizona!"

"What's da difference?" Dad said, "If we're goin' west, we might as well go all the way."

"I don't know, Herman. What about us?"

"I got it all figured out," Dad said. We'd heard that before, and it didn't sound good. "I'm going without you and the kids," he said. "Johnny and me are drivin'. I'll get a job and find a house, then I'll send fa youse."

That was it. We didn't have anything to say about it. Yeah, Mom was speechless. But she was powerless too.

A FEW DAYS LATER, Laura said she had figured out why Dad had to leave. But nobody told me anything. All I knew was that we weren't supposed to talk about California to anyone.

We had to cover for Dad while he was away. It wasn't easy because Freddie was hanging around so much he felt to us like a piece of the furniture. Freddie hung around the shoe shop, too. But Uncle Nick was there covering for Dad, and Nick wouldn't say anything. Laura said Freddie must have thought Dad had slipped town for a few weeks, until the heat cooled down. At first, she said he must have thought that Dad had gone to the dog races in Florida. Laura and Mom played it that way just to throw Freddie off.

Mom said she got some letters from Dad, but Laura and I

never saw any. Was she lying to protect us? She said everything was okay. She said he had gotten a job, and the money was good, but he was still looking for a house before he could send for us.

California was a dream for Laura and me. We wondered if we would ever see the Pacific Ocean, or if we'd ever see Dad again.

Mom wondered too. But as the time went by, we heard less and less from him; every time Mom got a letter, she told us Dad was still having a hard time finding a house. We kept thinking he eventually might just stop writing.

It was a bleak, lonely time; what Dad had promised would be a few weeks stretched on for nearly two months. We were surviving. And I'm sure Mom wasn't letting on how bad she saw the situation, when an envelope came in the mail. It was from Dad. He had found a place. And in the envelope, there were three airline tickets for a TWA flight from LaGuardia Airport to Los Angeles, California.

We felt like we were saved, but we still didn't know how we could get away from Freddie.

EVERY TIME WE TURNED AROUND, Freddie was there—on our way to school, on our way home. At the playground. Every few days we'd look out the kitchen window and see him sitting on the bench down on the block, reading the Racing Form. Or we'd find him leaning against the building, smoking a cigarette, or hiding in the alcove inside the entry door, lurking in the stairwell. Then jumping out at us.

"Herman in yet?" he'd say. "Where's Herman, kids? Laura, whatdaya know about ya fatha?"

We knew we should shut up, so we walked right by him, not saying a word.

We didn't know which way to turn. Should we start going over the roof like our father, just to avoid Freddie?

Finally, Mom realized that that might be the only way to

escape. But what were we to do with our furniture? Surely, he'd see us moving out. And what about our luggage? Maybe we should just leave the furniture there, write it off. But that wasn't an option. We had to do something to cover our trail.

Sure enough, Mrs. DeAngelo had a plan. She had studied the movements made by every neighbor, bill collector, and relative alike. And the "over the roof routine"? If someone went in but didn't come out, she'd say "they must have gone ova the pass."

That evening, half-a-dozen neighbors sat around the table drinking red wine, eating toasted bread rusks soaked in Anisette and popping lupini. They all spoke at once in a cacophony: "I'll move the lamps if you get the rugs." "It'll take four of us to get the sofa, two for the Victrola."

What were they doing? Were they thinking of carting the furniture up over the roof? A Chinese fire drill enacted by Italians in Long Island City? That's what Laura thought. But no one gave a clue. Anytime we'd ask, everyone would say, in concert, "Shut up. You don't need to know. You'll thank me later." So we shut up but tried to listen better. And when they saw us hanging around, someone would say, "Go down on the block. Make believe ya playing stoop ball. Let us know when Freddie arrives."

But to this day, I'm not sure if I'd only heard them fantasizing about what they wished they could do, or if I had done some serious fantasizing of my own. When Laura was still alive, I often told her about the stories I thought I had fabricated to make sense out of the chaos. But she'd often say "No, Joey, you didn't make it up. That's what really happened." Or maybe I've told myself this scenario so often I've come to believe it.

When the day came for our flight to California, Mrs. DeAngelo stood watch at her table as usual, as if nothing was going on. She would let us know when Freddie showed up. And she said she'd scream if Freddie got impatient smoking cigarettes on his bench and started to enter the apartment.

The neighbors formed a line from our front door at the apartment, twenty or thirty of them, stretching out the door, up the stairwell, over the roof and down the next apartment stairway.

Then it started. First the lamps, then the rugs. All the pictures from the walls, handed one-by-one down the line and out. Each and every piece of our furniture would be carried up, over and down again, dragged out around the corner, completely out of sight and onto a waiting truck where it would be taken to New Jersey and sold at the auction house where Cousin Johnny had already set up a deal. He'd handle it all and send us the money.

When Freddie showed up at around noon, he sauntered up slowly, so Mrs. DeAngelo shouted out the first warning.

"I'm making pasta fagiol tonight, Annie," Mrs. DeAngelo said. Mom understood what she meant: only when Ma heard Mrs. DeAngelo pronounce it Fazoo would she know that Freddie would be entering the building. When Mrs. DeAngelo said "fagiol" in her sing-song voice, Freddie must have looked up and snarled at how she pronounced it. But he must have been distracted, because Mom had told someone to leave the curtains up and she stood at the window and waved to give us cover. Our suitcases were packed, so we stood by and waited.

At that moment, Mrs. DeAngelo leaned out her window and said, "PASTA FAZOO," knowing that when Freddie did what he was now doing—lighting a cigarette and starting to pace and get fidgety—he'd soon be coming up. So we grabbed our luggage and headed left down the stairs, when Ma stopped us and said, "NO! The other way. We're going over the roof."

Meanwhile, Aunt Rose, just walking in, said, "Uncle Frank parked his Oldsmobile right around the block under the bridge and left the motor running so he could drive youse to the airport."

Mom and Laura and I all carried our own luggage. Now that Mom had left the window, Mrs. DeAngelo leaned out her apartment and said, "He's comin' in. I hope youse guys are well up the stairway. Betta hurry."

As we trudged up the stairs, Mom looked back and started to cry, especially when we climbed up the first flight of stairs as the fire drill carried our furniture toward the roof. Mom touched everything she passed—the sewing machine, the red Formica table, the chairs, the wringer washing machine. Uncle Frank tried to move her along so we could get out of there, but Mom had to have one last feel.

Mr. DeAngelo kept looking at his watch. According to the plan, all the furniture would be cleared out by 1 p.m., so that if Freddie found out, there would be enough time for us to make our flight. But the big stuff was causing problems. The sofa had to be stood up on end to make the turn in the stairwell, the Victrola took four men instead of two.

Eventually, everything was out of the apartment, everything except Mom's curtains and cornice and the bars on the kitchen window, just so Freddie didn't get suspicious until he actually entered the apartment.

Uncle Frank finally got Mom to move quicker, and we made it to the waiting car and headed for the airport. We heard that they were still moving furniture as we drove off.

We learned later that when Freddie started to enter the building, the last of the furniture was just on the floor above, so they started quietly shuffling the stuff remaining on each floor into neighbors' apartments. Seventh floor into the Glicklic's, eight floor into the Souza's, ninth floor into the McCreary's.

The neighbors hung out their kitchen windows and sighed every time Freddie moved, wondering when he'd finally go in to try and find Herman. Or if he ever would. Finally, Mr. DeAngelo exploded. He couldn't hold it anymore. By then he knew we were already gone. He blurted out, "Freddie, somet'in's goin' on in the Ortiz apartment." He ducked out of sight. Freddie looked around. By then he couldn't see who had yelled.

Freddie put out his cigarette, ran up the stairs, pushed open the door and saw nothing. The whole apartment was empty. Freddie stalked the apartment. He screamed at the top of his lungs, and his voice echoed, not just through the apartment and building, but out the window and through the blood-red canyons of the Queensborough Projects. Like everything that ever got explained, questioned, or analyzed through our kitchen window, everyone knew that we had escaped. Freddie ran out screaming in his Sicilian dialect, with everyone watching from their kitchen windows. No one ever saw Freddie again. At least no one in our old neighborhood.

On the way to the airport, my mother stopped at a Jewish haberdashery on Queens Boulevard and bought me—for who knows what reason—a full-length, gray wool overcoat. The coat came with a matching gray hat with flip down earmuffs. She said she didn't want me to catch cold.

When we got off of the plane in Los Angeles, the sun was blazing hot. It was 90 degrees and I must have looked like an Eskimo midget: a little Puerto Rican-Italian Eskimo in a gray wool overcoat who, with his mother and sister, had escaped from Queens to the bright, glaring sunshine of Southern California.

Who am I? – "the child is father of the man."

MY FATHER WAS A LIAR. *So, did I learn that from him? Or did I come by it on my own?*

Sometimes my practice of re-constructing a story is one of exploration—trying to observe what went on, then elaborating on it. Of course, Dad's ploy was different. That little glint in his eye when he told Mom about how he made ends meet, or that wink he shot Laura and me when Mom wasn't looking, may only have been his habit of "improving" on the truth, as he always said. Just the same, it must have taught me a ploy of my own.

I still don't know if certain events actually happened or if, after I heard someone joking about them (just like Dad's proverbial wink), they became real to my six-year-old mind. What I am positive of is that Freddie did show up that day unannounced to make book in our dining room. The image and powerful memory of the emotion of the scene has stuck with me all these years. And it was confirmed by Laura, who said that she knew for a fact that Dad had offered the apartment to settle a bet.

"It sounded just like Dad," she told me.

Years later, when I asked Rosemarie about the furniture-over-the-roof episode, she said she'd only heard rumors. Since her brother John Junior had "dealings" with auction houses and her father was a merchant marine at the time (both of them inclined to "moving goods," as they used to say), those two scenarios—the auctions and the shipping—seemed like logical explanations of the furniture sale.

But Laura was long gone from our lives when I wrote this detail of the furniture caper. So she couldn't let me know if I had been guilty of stretching the truth about the exact details of how we escaped Freddie's clutches.

Chapter Fourteen:
Palm Trees, Ice Cream Cones,
Tacos Puertorriqueños
& Orange Salad

DAD WAS SUPPOSED TO MEET US at the airport when we landed in California. I walked off the plane holding Mom's hand, using the other hand to shade the sun from my eyes. Before we could even get into the terminal, I started to whine and Mom could tell I was boiling up under my gray wool overcoat and fluffy hat with the built-in earmuffs.

"It's okay, Joey," Mom said. "Daddy will be here soon, and he'll carry your coat."

But Dad was nowhere to be seen. After picking up our luggage, we sat in the terminal for hours. It was like old times. Waiting for Dad. Laura and I started counting things as they went by. First sailors, then cowboy boots. Later we started slugging one another. Mom quickly got aggravated and twisted Laura's ear to make her stop.

Finally, Dad arrived as if nothing had happened. He'd gotten stuck in traffic, he said. He'd had to get gas. Always the deflection. We never knew if Dad would be there when we needed him. Mom put up with it; Laura and I had no choice.

On the way back from the airport we saw giant donuts and Paul Bunyan-sized tires, the oversized sculptures we'd heard about back in Queens but imagined only existed in Texas.

When we pulled into Wilmington, a small town at the edge of Los Angeles Harbor, it looked like paradise. Everything was clean and sparkling. Apartment buildings were painted in pastels of pink, salmon, and turquoise; forty-foot-tall palm trees swayed in the breeze. But the best thing we saw, right downtown, was the giant ice cream cone on top of Currie's Ice Cream Parlor. I thought the intense heat would melt the strawberry ice cream on top of the cone, but Laura said I was being stupid again. In any case, there it stood—bold and glistening. I wanted to climb up and start licking. And I wanted an ice cream so bad, but Mom said No.

While Dad stopped to get groceries, Mom explained to me that the giant tires and donuts, and even the ice cream cone, were all made of concrete. Sure, I was disappointed. The cones were not only fake, but I also didn't get to eat a real one.

In the back seat Laura looked at me, rubbed her fingers together and shook her head, as if it was about the money. Sure enough, Dad came out of Von's Supermarket holding a six-pack of beer and a bottle of whiskey in one arm. And in the other arm, he held a bag of groceries that looked paltry in comparison.

On the way from downtown to our new house, they all kidded me about thinking the giant sculptures were real. "Even so," Dad said. "You still gotta admit California's not Queens." The bright, new, bigger-than-life patina told us we were in for a new life, he said. We were free. And the possibilities were bigger than our imaginations. Even before we got to our new house we started to relax. The sunshine and clean air helped us shed that nagging fear that Dad was trapped and that we were being pulled down with him.

It was a new feeling that no one was after us. But would it hold?

The place Dad had found was a castle compared to our dingy apartment in the projects. First of all, it was a house. Our Aunt Margie and Uncle Frank lived in a house back in Flushing, but everyone else we knew lived in a projects apartment. Our new place had freshly painted walls, bright curtains, and windows that let the sunshine flood in every afternoon. It looked out onto a field—an oil field, but at least it was open space.

Everything seemed perfect until one day when Dad came home early from work, drunk and almost in tears. Mom sent me to bed even though it was early afternoon.

"Mom, it's still light out," I complained.

"I don't care," she said. "Go to bed."

I heard yelling. Dad got angry. I heard furniture and plates crashing in the living room. Mom was sobbing and Dad was getting louder and louder, and eventually I just stuffed the pillow over my head and fell asleep and blanked out.

The next day Dad started combing the real estate listings for a new house. He said he was looking for a cheaper place, but he would often stop reading the house ads and instead read out loud to Mom about shoe repair jobs in Fresno, Bakersfield, even Las Vegas. It seemed like we were always looking for something else. Maybe Dad had lost his job again. Or maybe he lost another piece of furniture in a bet. Or were we trying to cover our trail?

That evening Dad was sitting on the couch, cigarette and beer in hand, reading the classifieds.

"Nonnie," Dad yelled out to Mom. "I don't know how we're gonna find a new place. Every house and apartment in here that's cheap enough says, "Adults Only. No Pets. No Kids.""

He wadded up the paper and threw it on the couch with a disgusted look on his face and said, "What do they expect us to do with the kids . . . Drown them?"

"No, Daddy, No," I said. It was that same old fear of water covering over me again and the nightmare of drowning. I ran to Mom.

"Joey, Daddy's only kidding," Mom said, hugging me and rocking me protectively.

It brought back the memory of Dad's friend Eddie and his disappearance down by the East River. Maybe everything wasn't as safe as it seemed.

AFTER DAD HAD BEEN OUT OF WORK for a few weeks he went to Mom and asked her for $95, from the cash she'd earned from a job waiting tables at a local diner. Dad wouldn't tell Mom what it was for. "Not another deal, Herman."

She gave it to him reluctantly, and she really let him know she was upset because it was a whole week's tips and was supposed to last a month for groceries. She let Dad have the money only because she made him promise to pay back every nickel. Dad could be charming when it came to borrowing money and promising to pay it back. But when he took the money from Mom he acted like an animal groveling for scraps of meat. He made funny sounds under his breath as he took every cent Mom had—nickels, dimes, quarters, even pennies. He promised she'd get it back with interest.

And then he said, "I swear to ya, Nonnie, it'll never happen again."

Fortunately, Mom had been to the grocery that day and had already stocked up for the week. Besides eggs, toilet paper, milk, and hamburger, she had also bought a whole bag of California Sunkist navel oranges. Oranges were a symbol of California for us. Oranges. Their color, their perfect roundness, their shiny dappled skin. For some reason they called California the Golden State. Maybe it was because of the Gold Rush that happened a long time ago, or because of the color of the hills in summertime. But according to my sister, it was because of the oranges.

There were so many oranges in the market that season, and

they were so cheap, that Mom had to dig out an old peasant recipe she had learned from a Jewish lady who lived in Miami for
the winter. Mom peeled and cut up a few oranges into wedges
and put them into a shallow bowl. She covered the oranges with
a little olive oil and water, then sprinkled them with salt and
pepper. She added her own "California touch," as she called it:
a few leaves of fresh mint. Sounds strange, I know, though you
haven't heard the weirdest part (but have faith, it tastes delicious): something inside of me wants to say there was chopped
garlic in the dish. But I'm not sure. I know there weren't many
Jews around California to ask about it at that time, at least in
our neighborhood. And there weren't too many Puerto Ricans
either—except the one who couldn't resist telling Mom what
he thought of the dish. He stuck up his nose and told her that
oil and water don't mix. She must have known what he meant
because she didn't say a word.

Since Dad was free most days and Mom got off in the afternoon, we would all pile into Dad's old green Hudson and take
off for Hollywood. Dad's brother Johnny had started a new life
for his family as well, opening a restaurant just off Sunset Boulevard.

We learned later that the Sicilian gang in Queens got wind
of my father's escape to California because they heard about a
restaurant serving Puerto Rican food with an Italian twist. Freddie the bookie must have known that only a Puerto Rican from
Queens could concoct such strange combinations.

Uncle Johnny invented a dish that the rest of us called
Puerto Rican-Italian Tacos. It was Johnny's uncanny twist
of hand that made the dish special: you coat strips of chick-
en breast in tomato sauce and put them into corn tortillas
that are then deep fried. Open the shells slightly and add
some grated cheese, shredded lettuce, and diced tomatoes
on top.

Simple but good. He called them "Mexican Tacos, Italian Style" because, at the time, he didn't want to have anything to do with Puerto Rican. Customers always asked him if they could be called Chicken Cacciatore Tacos. And, sure, Johnny could buy that. As long as you didn't call them Puertorriqueño.

Dad was supposed to give Mom back the money he'd borrowed from her that night. But he made sure the trip to Johnny's diverted her attention by dancing, singing, and joking with Uncle throughout the evening.

As we started to leave the restaurant, though, Mom and Laura and I saw Dad quietly slide a fifty-dollar bill into Uncle Johnny's hand as they stood at the counter saying good-bye.

Dad and Mom argued about the money all the way back to Wilmington, while Laura and I counted the oversized sculptures along Sepulveda Boulevard—the hat on the Brown Derby Restaurant, the gigantic Dunkin' Donut, the Paul Bunyan-sized tires.

Dad hung onto a thread of responsibility for a while. He finally found work. And he gave Mom part of the $95 back. But he always finagled more money from her, sometimes without her even knowing it: he found out where she hid her tips and would often "borrow a few quarters," he said: "Just for smokes, Joey. Just for smokes."

There was always a shoe shop for him to work in, but no job lasted long. Money was always a problem. Money and drink. And eventually, he discovered the track. Maybe it was just that Santa Anita and Hollywood Park weren't in season when we had arrived. Who knows. But when the circuit finally came around, so did Dad. And the dreaded combination—booze, money, and horses—eventually led to his downfall.

Finally, Mom said she'd had enough. Maybe it was the $95 she never fully saw again. Maybe it was just everything all added up. Apparently, all the times he had "gone out of town" looking for work, Dad was only away because Mom had kicked him out. But she always took him back because he always begged. Or bought me a new football or a bow and arrow to get me on his side, so Mom would take pity on him.

I think by my own count, it took maybe five or six times. I think we'd heard about the cockroach story from the health inspector down at the cafe. You exterminate them once or stomp on them in the storeroom, but they just keep bouncing back, resurrecting themselves. You do it over and over again, but they keep springing back into your life . . . a recurring pest. Impossible to kill.

Who knows why Mom put up with it. Laura and I had no choice. But finally one day, Mom had had enough. She said it was over.

"Joey," she finally said. "I had to tell Daddy to leave."

"Oh no, Mom. Again?"

It must have been more than the $95. Maybe it was him "borrowing a few dollars" from the till or taking beers from the café fridge. But that all seemed so small compared to how his erruptions would cause us all to go catatonic with fear.

"He's not coming back this time," she said. "Now we have to be even more careful."

"I'm sorry, Mom. I'll be good."

"It's not your fault," Mom said. "But we have to make it on our own from now on."

Self-blame

THE "CHILDHOOD GUILT OF SELF-IMPOSED AGENCY" is a phrase that popped into my head one day years later while going through my own self-therapy in writing this memoir as well as working with a therapist. For me it expresses the idea that as kids we often blame ourselves when we fall prey to the comments, well-meaning wishes, and actions of others—mostly adults. When my long-time dedicated editor Sarah Rabkin asked in an editing note, "And we do this be-cause?" my answer came out in a rant:

> *Because we're fucking kids, that's why! And we've been put down, told what to do, told to behave a certain way even though we see those same adult assholes behaving bad-ly themselves. And them wanting to be in control because they're bigger than us and they know more, and because they're smarter, and they've been through it so they know from experience, and they hold all the cards, and "It's better for us," and "You'll thank us later," and "You're too young to understand." And fa chrissakes, WE JUST BELIEVE IT.*

AFTER THE RANT IS OVER, I collect myself and try to understand that Sarah was right in asking me to explain it. And then feeling guilty all over again, and overwhelmed by, well, that it was my fault in the first place. Exaggerating the same feeling of "the childhood guilt of self-imposed agency." A vicious cycle.

Even though I think I came up with the term myself, not having read it somewhere in some psychology book or essay, or not having heard it from one of my many therapists over the years, I feel it must be a concept practitioners are aware of. Those assholes have some-thing to say about everything. And they know it all too. (There I go again.)

So, "shut up," I tell myself. It must be a natural thing for kids to take on guilt (maybe to please their parents?). And who knows if the adults who are "laying it on us" even know they're doing it.

Is that how the phrase, "breaking the cycle" grows out of the notion of a desire to escape our parents' harmful habits?

Chapter Fifteen:
Lost Wages and Found Cauliflower

AFTER DAD WAS FINALLY GONE, we lost track of him for more than a few months. He wasn't suddenly showing up at awkward times, making us wonder if he was going to try and beg Mom to let him stay, or weasel his way back into our lives.

We started to hear rumors that he had taken a job in Fresno or Bakersfield and that he might be doing all right for himself. But when we heard he was working up in Lompoc or Atascadero, and whenever any of our neighbors would be talking to Mom about it, they would snicker. And if I walked in, they would change the subject. Truth was that Lompoc and Atascadero both have minimum security facilities, but no one ever told me that, although Mom and Laura must have known.

Months later we heard that Dad was in Las Vegas, and the minute Mom heard, she just shook her head and said, "Vegas and your father deserve one another."

Dad would visit us on occasion, and each time we were less fearful that he might try to move back in. He looked straight and clean-cut for a change. He wasn't wearing the navy-blue pants and black shoes or all the browns and grays he had always worn in Queens. One time he was wearing a pair of pleated, cream-colored pants and two-tone Oxfords that reminded me of the ones Eddie had worn the day he came back from Florida. The shoes had that fine netting that showed off Dad's new silk socks. The socks confused us. Socks had never figured in Dad's life before. Did this mean he was wearing underwear too? I'm sure Mom never wanted to find out.

We never knew how long he'd stay or how close he would get. I don't think anyone ever found out about the underwear. I know I never did. And we could tell that he and Mom were truly separated because Dad always slept on the couch.

The last night of his first visit, after having disappeared for so long, was like old times. Mom made rice and beans for Dad and fried up some chicken cutlets. Although Dad had brought a big bottle of Chianti with the straw basket around the bottom, he didn't have a drink of it. There weren't the half-dozen or so quarts of Rheingold or Pabst that Dad used to polish off, then pile into the garbage. He did have a few cigarettes, but this time there were no crumpled-up packages spread all over the place like there used to be—only a few smelly ashtrays scattered around the house.

Dad started talking about Vegas and that he wanted to bring me there. I could swim in the Muni pool, he said, and visit for a week before the start of baseball, or drive with him out to the desert for sunsets. Mom listened but didn't make a peep.

Like before, Dad made promises. He had talked about the horse races and promised to take me to the track so often that it became one of those fantasies that ruled my life. Back in New York he had always promised to take me to see the Dodgers, but he never came through. When we first made it out to California I started to believe he might take me to Santa Anita or Hollywood Park. But now it was too late. And, as Laura said later, everything Dad promised was an attempt at convincing Mom to let him back into our lives.

On that first visit, Dad brought us presents from Las Vegas.

He brought me a one-armed bandit that took real coins. He even gave me a roll of nickels to run through the machine. He brought Laura an Everly Brothers record: "Johnny is a Joker, he's a dog. Johnny took my honey, he's a bird. He's a bird dog." Over the rice and beans and cutlets, we talked about the six huge heads of cauliflower Dad had brought for Mom. He knew she liked to prepare it the way her mother had taught her, by cutting the florets into small pieces, dipping them in egg batter, and frying them in hot olive oil.

Dad said he had bought the cauliflower at a roadside produce stand on the highway that runs through the Mojave Desert. "They're a little bruised, Nonnie," Dad said, "because they rolled around in the trunk all the way back.

"You shoulda seen the faces of da inspectors at the state line when I told 'em I had a dead body in the trunk." Mom and Laura looked at one another and smirked. Would Dad ever change?

Still, there was more evidence that he was getting his life together. He started talking about the Baha'i Faith. Anyone who knew Dad understood that the only time he prayed in his life was the night Freddie showed up with the gun, or maybe the night he squatted behind the counter when both Eddie and Freddie showed up looking for the same pair of shoes. Dad had been baptized and raised a Catholic, but like he always said, "I used to be Catholic, but I gave it up for Lent." So, it was hard for us to believe he had gotten religion in the desert.

Dad had brought a book with him that looked like a strange bible. He talked about 'Abdu'l Bahá, the group's spiritual leader, and how this man, this prophet, was still alive during Dad's own lifetime. "He was in New York the day Johnny and I arrived from Puerto Rico," he told us.

He said he had met many nice people attached to the Baha'i church who all wanted to help him. Then he mentioned someone named Alice and his eyes lit up. This seemed odd to me at

147

the time—I guess because I always thought Mom would eventually let him come back home again— but to Laura and Mom it had a calming effect. It relaxed the evening even more. It must have meant that Dad was finally creating a life for himself.

"When I first got to Vegas," Dad said, "the people in the Baha'i Faith said, 'You shouldn't call it Las Vegas at all. If you didn't consider it "Lost Wages" you wouldn't last very long, because you wouldn't be able to handle the temptation." So from then on we all called it Lost Wages.

"Speaking of Lost Wages, Nonnie," Dad said, "I think ya should let me take Joey with me this time."

There was a big silence.

"Ya wanna go, doncha, Joey?" Dad said.

I started to get excited. "I don't know, Herman," Mom said, which usually meant No.

"What do you think I'm gonna do," Dad said, "teach him to gamble? Stuff him in the trunk?"

We all laughed. It must have loosened Mom up, because she started to get a smile on her face. So, Dad went on, "Take him out into the desert, dig a big hole and . . ."

"HERMAN!" Ma yelled, "You're starting to aggravate me . . ." So Dad stopped. Ma turned her sneer back into a half-smile. Still, Dad's habit of taking a joke too far and Mom's snarly reaction was like old times. And brought back the old memories—for all of us.

"He'll like Alice," Dad said. "And she wants ta meet him. And Joey can go swimmin' every day while I'm at work. If he goes wit me tomorrow, I can have him back in a week for baseball."

"Oh, you're coming back in a week?" Ma said.

"I'd have to. You want him back, don't you?"

"Yeah, Herman!" Ma said. "I want him back."

I was jumping out of my seat, but Mom was only swaying back and forth a little, the way she would when she was pondering one of Dad's schemes or protecting me. She knew I wanted to go.

"Okay," she said. "But you have to have him back next Sunday." What she meant was, one week and then you'd better bring him back, or else.

And Dad understood.

WE PULLED INTO LOST WAGES as the sun was going down; it was just dark enough to see all the million glittering neon lights on the Strip.

"This city never sleeps," Dad said. "They call it gaming but it's really gambling." I wasn't sure what that meant, but later that night, after we had a bowl of chili 'n' beans with saltine crackers at a diner near Dad's shoe shop, he took me downtown and I found out. Dad drove me right under the sign over Fremont Street that reads, "Welcome to Fabulous Downtown Las Vegas," and, for the first time, I experienced the city's overwhelming glitz. I was afraid and excited all at once. It was also the first time I saw the giant "Howdy Podner" neon cowboy outside the Nevada Club that made the giant donuts, tires, and ice cream cones in California look tame in comparison.

Inside the Golden Nugget, there were card tables, dice tables, slot machines. The so-called gaming that Dad had always done in the dim-lit alley behind the shoe shop back in Queens went on for real in a glittery, dramatically-lighted place.

"Yep, Joey," Dad said. "There dey are, all those lost souls. And they're here all night, some of 'em. The only time anyone goes home is when they lose all their money."

With Dad holding onto my hand, we strolled around the tables and down a couple of aisles of slots, then we headed right back out the same door we had come in.

"There," he said, "Ya seen it. The hopeless souls. But not me. Ya daddy don't gamble no more. Let's go home."

Home was the back of the shoe shop, a lot like Dad's shop in Queens, except more permanent: a little couch, a table, and a cot behind the partition. The seediest reminder of Dad's arrangement was a hotplate in the corner, out of the way, but a fixture, not only for heating soup but for mixing Dad's concoctions for fixing scars on expensive shoe leather.

As Dad threw a blanket on the cot for me and set up the couch for himself, he started to get excited talking about Alice, and since he hadn't been drinking, it wasn't like the stories he had told in the bars back in Queens or on the subway to Coney. That's how I felt safe that I was with Jokester Herman, who wouldn't easily slip into Volcano Herman.

"Joey, I think she likes me," Dad said. And we fell off to sleep talking about Alice to the blinking lights of the downtown Casinos and the swinging arm of the neon "Howdy Pardner" statue that stood 40 feet high over Lost Wages.

BEFORE I COULD RUN OFF to the Muni swimming pool the next morning, Alice showed up. Just like Dad had said, she was enthusiastic, bright, and of course pretty. I could see why Dad thought Alice liked him; she was tuned in to everything. After we talked a few minutes, things got uncomfortable because I wanted to go. Dad started ribbing me, just like the old days, when he told her, "Joey's a pretty fart smeller, Alice." At first I thought Alice didn't catch the joke. But quickly, she turned to Dad and said, "Well, look who his father is."

Dad let out a muffled laugh, turned down his lips and scrunched up his shoulders. It was the last time I ever heard him use that phrase. I'm not sure if Dad ever realized that Alice was just ribbing Dad right back. She was smart. And pretty cool at that.

It made me wonder: Was it religion that was speaking to him, or was it the fact that he had the hots for Alice, those uncontrollable urges that always ruled his life? Dad always embarrassed me when he talked to girls. He would pump his eyebrows and smile that wicked smile. He would nudge me and do that clicking sound with his tongue as if I knew what the hell he was thinking. But I never knew because he never told me.

It was one of the reasons that, secretly, I always wished Dad would get himself lost for good and never find his way back.

As promised, Dad eventually did let me go to the Muni plunge and swim all morning. It became my ritual for the next six days. At night Dad and I would go to the diner for chili, or we'd take a pizza back to the shoe shop or open a can of soup and heat it on the electric burner.

When the week was over, on Saturday afternoon, we got into the Hudson and headed back to Wilmington. Just before the state line, around 9 p.m., on a barren stretch of road, Dad yelled out, "Oh, boy," pulled the car over and swerved to a stop. He got out of the car and went around back of the abandoned gas station. When he came back moments later, he held a huge head of cauliflower in each hand. "Got these at the produce stand, Joey. Don't tell Mommy."

What produce stand? I only saw old, rusty gas pumps, a barren highway, an empty field.

* * * *

THE NEXT TIME DAD VISITED us was months later. He didn't look so good. He had a two-day growth, an old pair of navy-blue slacks on, and his wingtips with no socks. He didn't say a word about Alice, and none of us were about to ask. When he talked about work or Nevada or getting back on his feet, all he did was mumble "Lost Wages" and shake his head. Whenever he called it Lost Wages, we knew Dad might be rebounding off of some recent binge in which he had lost a lot of money and he had decided to start calling it by its funny name—as a religious chant or something—just to get himself back on the right track.

Mom's face expressed her disgust when he showed up that time. Even so, she let him talk her into driving us up to Johnny's for a visit. On the way I counted palm trees. Early in the drive, Dad pulled over to a liquor store and bought a quart of beer. We couldn't tell if it was Pabst or Rheingold because he kept it in the bag and held it between his legs, taking an occasional sip as he drove.

Dad smoked cigarette after cigarette until the ashtray overflowed. He got more and more excited and talkative. But Mom was quiet. She just stared out the window. I guess she was counting palm trees, too.

Finally, Dad leaned over the back seat and told me something he might once have said to me in private but never with Mom around: "Joey, whatever ya wanna do in life, I'll be proud of ya.

"But whatever ya do, be good at it. Even if ya decide to become a crook. Be a good crook."

Mom was appalled. We were in the car somewhere near Uncle Johnny's place in Hollywood, because it happened when we were passing the Brown Derby Restaurant. And like those giant donuts, oversized tires, and ice cream cones, the large brown concrete hat was a reminder that things out here were bigger than life, outlandish, fanciful. They pointed directly to the very idea that Dad had always based his life on: " . . . if you're gonna do something, do it big and brash. If you're supposed to go to Arizona, why not go all the way to the Coast? And if ya can't pull it off, ya just have to take the consequences."

"Consequences." Not a word you would expect to hear out of the mouth of a Puerto Rican peasant from the jungles outside of San Juan, who had survived on the streets of New York, had come within inches of losing his life in Queens, had escaped with his family to California, and eventually had joined the Baha'i Faith in a strange desert oasis called Lost Wages. But in that Puerto Rican patois of his it all rang true. It clicked and rang off his tongue like all the other fancy words he used. And even though Mom wanted to kill him for making a comment about me becoming a "good" crook, she knew that as long as he was far removed from our lives, out in the desert somewhere, tolerating Dad was the best she could do. She had taken him for who he was all those years. Of course, I had always suppressed the visions of his reaching for his belt or clenching his fist and coming at me. But now I was safe, both bodily and emotionally, from Dad's bad influence. And that was all she cared about.

DAD CAME BACK A FEW MORE TIMES during my teenage years, but his visits were separated by long stretches of absence. He always brought food for Mom to cook, mostly cauliflower or broccoli. "Lost Wages don't have no spaghetti and meatballs, Nonnie," he told her. "There's dis produce stand outside Bishop where they sell dis stuff. And it's cheap." Then he winked at me.

As usual, Laura pulled me aside and told me the real story: Dad had found the cauliflower on the side of the road, where it had fallen off the trucks that took them to the big produce market in Central L.A. He never bought a thing. That's why there were always more than we could eat. That's why they were always bruised.

Mom made use of them, though. She never let anything go to waste. We ate steamed cauliflower; cauliflower casserole with anchovies, pine nuts, raisins, and breadcrumbs; we ate cauliflower with garlic and tomatoes as a sauce for pasta; we ate cavolfiore fritti alla parmigiana, the fried florets I told you about that Mom made the night Dad had showed up wearing socks. Try it with some anchovy mayonnaise. Not too healthy, I know, but it'll make you feel good, especially if you've been eating steamed cauliflower all week. Or if you've been bruised or shamed by an uncaring father.

Ever hear the expression, "We ate it until we had it coming out of our ears"? Well, Mom knew all the recipes. It may have taken two weeks, but we ate cauliflower every day until it was gone. It made the memory of Dad linger on long after we managed to rid him from our lives for good.

Soon, I hoped.

The monkey in me, the paintbrush & the quarters

I WAS A MIMIC, A MONKEY. When Dad had been thrown out of the house and had moved to Las Vegas, Mom let me visit him for a few weeks in summer. One day we went into a hardware store where I saw him look around, survey the check-out boy at the register, pick up a cheap paintbrush. and simply put it in his pocket when he thought I wasn't looking. He quickly turned his head toward me, then toward the door, motioning for us to leave. Nothing else said.

Later that week we went to a fireworks show and he gave me a few bills to buy a hot dog and Coke. When the vendor mistakenly gave me too much change, I threw the few extra quarters into my pocket, feeling they were all mine, just as Dad had pocketed the paintbrush. When I showed my father the coins, he erupted. "You go right back there and tell him you were wrong," he said. "And give it all back." Dutifully, I slunk back and felt like crap.

It's important to state that the paintbrush experience happened before Dad discovered his new religious belief, while the encounter with the quarters happened shortly after he had found the Baha'i Faith in Las Vegas. So surely, his reprimand had come from his newly found religion. But his same old habits always seemed to re-surface, and that must have forced me to resent him for influencing me through his actions.

But was it my own fault? I kept being reminded of my newly-dis-covered idea of the "childhood guilt of self-imposed agency" forcing kids to feel guilt over their parents' actions. Therapists say that one form of child abuse is a co-dependence forced upon us by our parents' need to be comforted in some way. ("Go get me a beer, Joey.")

At twelve years old, I didn't have the self-knowledge or confidence to understand why I felt shame. My father's hypocrisy is what still weighs on me.

Only now do I realize why I felt so worthless. For years, mirroring his behavior became a blind habit. To have been shamed that evening for mimicking his actions threw a disturbing blanket of embarrassment over me. Now I can see why I may have been trying to make him proud. But I'm learning to see his duplicity as a neglectful action that made me feel confused and worthless.

Chapter Sixteen:
My Life as a Waitress

AFTER WORKING HER TAIL OFF for years as a waitress at a truck stop called Henry's Café—where she had learned how to mesmerize oil riggers, boat builders, and longshoremen with a hamburger and a bottle of Pabst Blue Ribbon beer—Mom gained the confidence and extra money to open her own place.

Dad was finally gone, and we'd only heard from him sporadically for a long time—so Mom didn't have to worry about him putting his hand in the till or grabbing free beers every ten minutes. She opened a twelve-stool burger hut she called Ann's Café, located in a ramshackle wooden building with hundreds of windows and bright-yellow peeling paint. The café stood on the corner of "B" and Broad Streets, right in the bowels of the L.A. Harbor, where the rank aroma of the fish canneries mixed with the burnt smell of copra on ships arriving from South America. Ann's Café was nestled in among the boatyards that built big ferrocement hulls, with a clear view of the San Pedro hills to the southwest.

As Dad had said with sour grapes when Mom told him about her idea for the café, it was "sink or swim" for us, and Mom couldn't afford to hire extra help, so both Laura and I became Mom's crew. We all quietly knew it was better to try and survive

*Mom and Me in the cornfield right next to our
second rental house in Wilmington.*

on our own than have Dad around to drag us down. Still, it was
a struggle. There was no such thing as wages; even the tips went
to Mom and "the family." We were in this thing together.

I worked at Ann's Café every summer day after playing baseball down at Harbor Park. After the games, I would slip my
baseball glove over the handlebar of my bike and pedal furiously
for twenty minutes to get to work, arriving at the café sweaty
and out of breath just before lunch.

In the beginning, Mom taught me general chores, like how to sweep and mop. I chopped onions and soaked the beans for chili. Chili was Mom's specialty. I don't think my mother had even heard of chili 'n' beans when we left New York for California six years earlier. Now she was the chili queen of the L.A. Harbor.

After the customers were gone, I cleared plates and wiped counters, and after that I'd wash dishes. The job I hated most came at the end of the day: the dirty-dishrag routine. We had several buckets filled with Clorox and suds, and we'd wring the rags out and pass them from bucket to bucket before we finally rinsed them clean, then hung them over the sink to dry.

Although I wore Levi's and dusty sneakers and always arrived wearing my baseball cap, Mom had me trained to tuck in my shirt and slick down my hair. When I finally learned not to scratch my nose and wipe my mouth and I started to gain a little confidence, Mom let me wait on customers.

But before the lunch rush, I made the "setups" for the burgers. In a little assembly line we created to make Mom's orders go smoothly, I'd layer the lettuce, tomato, onion, and pickle in neat little stacks on her worktable. I got them all lined up in rows so that, when the rush came, all Mom had to do was scoop them onto the spatula and slide them onto the grilled burger and bun.

As the guys started coming in, I took their orders and handed them back over the partition between the café and kitchen to Mom. Joking with all those "galoots," as Mom would call them, was the hardest part. But only because I didn't know them. I was shy with strangers, but with anyone I'd gotten to know even halfway, I'd try out my imitation-Jerry Lewis routine—often smooshing up my face, squeaking out indiscernible words and phrases, and even falling on the floor. Mom didn't enjoy these fits of self-expression. She never knew when I'd crawl back into my shell if some stranger said "boo" to me the wrong way.

These guys were hard to figure. They didn't eat spaghetti very often. They didn't know what a Chocolate Egg Cream was. They called soda "pop." They didn't call coffee "black coffee" or "brown coffee" like we did in New York. They just called it mud.

After getting to know their habits—and lingo—I got loose enough to jive with them. But it backfired. Now that I started playing along, kibbitzing about work, and joking about food, they started to shove the ribbing right back at me. One day a guy named Harry from Ets-Hoken Electrical next door came in and said, "You're a pretty good waitress, kid." Everybody laughed. It was what my mother was afraid of—me becoming worthless to her by becoming shy and silent. I fought it for a few days, but when I realized that their jokes just got worse, I stopped complaining and started to play along. And as Dad would have said, "Ya gotta do something to change ya luck." So, I started imitating what the guys were saying: "Waitress, another pop please." Or "Hey Toots, how about another cup 'a mud?" Whether I'd make it as a seasoned waitress or not, I couldn't tell. I was still just a twelve-year-old kid working in a lunch hut, pushing greasy burgers at gruff and sweaty longshoremen who wanted their food dished up as raunchy as they were.

THIS GUY NAMED BILL, for example, always asked for a burger with a greasy bun. That's where Mom had to put the bun on the griddle next to the beef patty as it cooked so it got splattered by the sizzling juices. You might expect a longshoreman or truck driver to order a burger with a greasy bun—but Bill was a freight expediter. While most of our customers stank from loading cargo or working on oil rigs and wore ratty clothes and a two-day stubble, Bill was slick and well-scrubbed and wore a white shirt, tie, and slacks.

One day I was bussing tables and I had about a dozen spoons, cups, and saucers tangled up in my hands. Bill was sitting behind me next to the cash register. He leaned over and touched my arm and said: "You know, from the side you look just like Herman."

I immediately spun around and sent saucers and silverware flying everywhere, splattering a few customers, unnerving several others. Mom seemed to put up with my occasional accidents because I was "good free help." But this time it was different. Bill's comment threw me off balance. How did he know what Dad looked like? I avoided him after that. I couldn't tell if Bill was just one of Dad's California drinking buddies, or if he had been sent by someone from New York—to hunt Dad down. A few days later Laura told me that Bill was trying to get to know Mom. Laura said that when Bill came around to yak with her after closing, Mom had shown him some snapshots from New York. So that's how he knew all about us.

When we got to know Bill and he started to come over to the house, we found out he had been a prizefighter. One day out in the backyard, he taught me how to hold up my dukes, how to make a left jab and a right cross—more practical information in a fifteen-minute lesson than I ever got from Dad in twelve years of horsing around.

A FEW DAYS AFTER the flying-silverware incident, right in the middle of the lunch rush, two men we'd never seen before came in and greeted Bill as if they knew him. They grabbed stools next to him at the counter. Like Bill, they were better dressed than our usual customers. In fact their broad pinstripe suits seemed out of place in our area of the Harbor.

I had arrived twenty minutes late because my game had gone into extra innings and—like I tried to tell Mom—I knew I was going to get to bat in the bottom of the 10th and couldn't let the team down. She didn't buy it. And because I was late, the setups for the burgers weren't ready. The dirty dishrags were still fermenting in their buckets. The dishrag smell was starting to float out from the shed, in through the back door of the diner, and throughout the café.

My foul-up put Mom behind for the whole day. She sweated more than usual just trying to keep up. Like me, Mom must have known the mystery of the two guys would get answered later.

At the most hectic time in the lunch rush, my basketball buddy, Manny Perez, ran in to pick me up for practice. Mom liked Manny because he had good manners, she said, and because he came from a decent Mexican family. Manny was bright and outgoing, always willing to offer a smile or tell a story. He enjoyed doing you a favor without your even asking; or he'd offer you a glaring observation. Manny could tell I was behind and flustered but, as usual, he blurted out exactly what was on his mind: "I think I saw your father on a bus from Reno," he said. "Is he moving back in?"

Mom, Laura, and I—all at opposite ends of the café—raised our heads and looked at one another. If they were thinking what I was thinking, we were all in trouble: was Dad trying to finagle his way back into our lives again?

At the same time the two strangers gave each other odd looks. They both got up at the same time, put down some money and left. Bill stayed in his seat, quietly chomping on his greasy burger.

Lunch wound down quickly, so Mom made a burger for Manny and gave him some fries and a Coke. I was getting nervous about the two strangers and about Dad and wanted to get out of there. Mom knew I wanted to go to practice. Even so, she made me help her prep the burger patties for the next day. I felt trapped, like I was underwater and being held down.

Mom mixed a big bowl of ground beef together with some chopped onions, salt, and pepper. Then she threw in a "couple eggs" and some grated Parmesan cheese. She shaped the ground beef into balls with an ice cream scoop and placed each one on a piece of wax paper. I could see the anguish in her face. I'm sure she could feel my anguish, too. Or I hoped so. I wanted out of there. For some weird reason, none of us wanted to see Dad again. Maybe I still dreaded a repeat of the last time he shamed and embarrassed me in front of my friends. Always joking. Always ribbing me. Maybe it was something else I was too afraid to remember. I'm sure Mom and Laura had their own reasons for not wanting to see him.

Hurry up, Mom, I thought. I've got to go. But still, she made me prep the burger patties for the next day, giving me that look that said *stay right here and help!*

I covered each ball of ground beef with another sheet of wax paper, then—with a heavy whack—I flattened each one with a large can of Italian plum tomatoes. I don't know if it made a difference if it was tomatoes in the can, but I do know that a number ten can was the best size to use for shaping burgers, crushing garlic, and throwing at mice in the storeroom. I was so charged up about possibly seeing Dad again that I wanted to take a hook shot right into the garbage with one of the cans. I wanted out of there. And Manny was almost done with his burger.

Burgers were soul food for truck drivers, longshoremen, and kids, too, as you could tell by how Manny was inhaling his. These lumps of greasy meat had crunchy edges. When we shaped them, some of the ground meat would squeeze out from under the can to form an irregular border of crunchy bits of beef when they were fried on the hot griddle.

Suddenly, Manny stood up, thanked Mom for the burger and fries and headed toward the door. Maybe this would convince Mom that I had to leave. But at that moment an office worker from the neighborhood walked in and ordered six burgers to go, and Mom had to work like hell to get it done. She nodded her head at me as a demand that I stay right there and help. Just then one of the strange guys came back in without our knowing it and peeked over the partition that separated the kitchen from the counter. Mom had one of the setups on her spatula just ready to put on the bun when the guy said:

"Can you make that a chili size?"

Mom jumped. The lettuce, tomato, onion, and pickle went flying. She must have thought he would be asking about Dad.

"A chili size," Mom said, trying to look calm. "What's that?"

"It's an open-faced burger on a bun," the guy said. "Then you smother it with chili and beans."

Mom nodded, so the guy took a seat.

"These Californians," my mother said. "He scared the hell outta me." Well, he scared the shit out of me, too, but I couldn't say it out loud or Mom would have smacked me.

"Leave it to these galoots to come up with a name like 'chili size'," Mom said to me. We never figured out what it meant.

Mom brought the chili size to the counter; the guy asked Mom to sit down. I couldn't hear what was going on. But I started sweeping and made my way closer. Mom had a pained look on her face.

Just then Manny, still at the door and waiting, started to get fidgety. He said, "Common, Joe, we've got to get to practice." He tried to drag me out of there. Part of me wanted to go. But I was also dying to find out what was going on with Mom and the guy. "Mom, is Dad coming back?" I said. But Mom was talking intently to the guy, who kept asking questions. "What is it, Ma? Is it okay?"

"It's okay, Joey," she said, "Your fatha doesn't live in Vegas anymore. Everything is fine. He's even further away. So don't worry." Was she lying to make me feel better? Her leery look and strange eye contact with "the guy" made me wonder, uneasily. Her eyes dropped down to the counter. She had a stoic look on her face and, as always happened, the closer I got to knowing the real story, the less I wanted to know—especially if she didn't want to talk about it, and it had something to do with Dad.

"Go, Joey, go," Mom said. "Go to practice." Manny had run out without me for what seemed like an eternity before I could get out of there. I thought he might leave me behind.

At that moment, just like clockwork, Bill walked in. He sat with the chili size guy and waited for Mom.

Laura was there, hovering over the counter, polishing glasses and listening in. And she just waved at me to get out of there. Anytime I could escape, I would. And this was the perfect time. I ran out like a waitress in a Las Vegas diner getting off for the weekend. I threw my apron in the basket and ran for the door, saying, "Bye Ma, bye Laur," and was gone. Manny was already on his bike, his kickstand up, when I got outside and grabbed my bike. But as we were ready to ride off, Manny blurted out, "I thought you said your Dad was still in Las Vegas?"

"What do you mean?" I said.

"That was him on the bus. He was just here. When he saw your mom and the guy talking to Bill, your dad got this wild look on his face and ran off to get something in his car."

DAD WALKED UP twirling a basketball on his fingertip.

"Get outta here, Manny," I said. "I'm gonna be late for practice. Go on. I mean it. Go." I hadn't seen Dad for months. I didn't know what the hell was going on or what he had in mind, but I knew I didn't want Manny to hear what might happen next.

"This ball's for you, Joe," Dad said, with an unsteady, groveling tremor in the bottom of his throat. I'd heard it before and it made me go catatonic. "Who's that guy in there?" Dad said. "What's he talking to Mom about? I'm worried, Joey. Aren't you?"

I was starting to feel shittier and shittier. I didn't want to be there. It was like confession, talking to the priest behind the screen in the confessional. Only this time, having to tell your Dad that your Mom now had a friend. A very close friend. So I shut up.

"Please talk to Mommy, Joe," Dad said. "Tell her to let me come home."

I didn't say anything. I felt sorry for him. Still, I knew if he came back, he'd bring the misery again. I tried not to say anything that would make him explode, but saw the look in his eyes—the erupting volcano.

"Why didn't you stick up for me, Joey?" Dad said. "I'm ya fatha. Help me out."

"Dad, I will," I said, not knowing where that came from. "But later. I gotta go now. You wouldn't want me to be late for practice." So I jumped on the bike and sped off, with Dad still standing there—him and the basketball.

"Joey, Come back. Let me explain something. Joey."

I circled around to sneak back into the café to warn Mom and heard Dad yelling after me.

"Get your ass off that bike, Mister! Listen to me. I'm your father."

Just then Bill left Mom in the café and walked out. I saw him through the hundred windows encountering Dad. And Laura, Mom, and I saw them wave their arms wildly and exchange muffled screams that none of us could hear. Then Mom went out and asked Bill to leave. And Dad must have pleaded with Mom, to convince her to let him come back home for good again. I can only guess at what they were saying; but I had seen and heard it at least a half dozen times before, so I imagined it went something like this:

Mom picked up the basketball and shook it in Dad's face. Dad must have confronted Mom about her new relationship with Bill because Laura and I heard Dad say, "I saw you in there talking to him. It's bad for Joey."

"I know what you're doing, Herman," Mom said, "You're using the basketball to get him back on your side. So don't try to change the subject by bringing up Bill. He's a customer."

She told Dad it was no use. That it could stay the way it had been—the occasional visits. And I'd heard that a half dozen times too.

Dad's face got more and more contorted.

Mom said: "Besides, Herman, I know what's bad for my son. I'll let you come home to see him from time to time. But I can't let you come back."

Then Dad waved for me to come out. At first I refused. But I'd learned to listen to him, or else.

"Tell your mutha, Joey. Tell her you want me to come home."

He pleaded with me, but again I went silent.

"Leave him alone, Herman," Mom said. "It's too late." She turned and walked back toward the café. She saw me start to cry even though I tried to hold it back.

"I'm going inside; I'm leaving, Herman. And you better leave too."

And I was there with Dad alone. The moment Mom left, Dad exploded, and the crying got worse. My sobbing was too much for Dad, who turned on me, his anger starting to rage.

I held onto my bike ready to leave.

"Where's the basketball?" he said, his voice softening but still holding that foreboding rumble that I feared so much. He convinced me to walk with him into the alleyway behind the café. I could feel his anger rising. Suddenly, an image of Dad putting his hands on his belt flashed before my eyes.

"Hit you," I said and mimicked him by raising my hand impulsively. And he exploded. I saw his fists clench, his jaw tighten. He found the ball and kicked it into the back shed. I started to cry even more, and followed the ball in there, not knowing what was coming. I picked up my bike and held onto it as if it was a shield. But it was no use.

"Stop crying," he said. But I couldn't stop. I tripped over my bike, broke a few spokes, and tumbled down onto the dirt. And he started swinging at me. First one smack and then another, each time saying, "Boys don't cry. Boys don't cry." And another smack right on the face: "Boys don't cry." After several more hits, with me unable to stop sobbing, I blacked out. When I came to, my crying turned to deep, drawn-out sobs. And then into hyperventilating. Then gasping for breath, practically suffocating myself in order to stop balling. But I did. I finally stopped. And so did he.

The basketball had bounced out of the shed and back to him. He nudged it at me with his foot. And then he turned around and walked a few paces away. And there I was with the bike and the basketball and my embarrassment all alone.

He just stood there, his back to me, his arms crossed, staring out at the L.A. Harbor.

I heard Laura from inside: "Ma, you have to go out there. It's happening again. You have to stop it." But it was too late.

Mom came out, cradled me in her arms, and held my wet, swollen face to hers. She dried what remained of the tears. Quickly, she confronted Dad: "It's all over" she said, squinting at the rage on Dad's face. "You can't come home. Ever again. Not to the house, not here. I'm never letting you near Joseph again."

A MOMENT LATER, I walked by the hundred windows of the diner and saw Mom and Laura at the counter consoling one another. Mom was forlorn. She glanced out at me in a strange way. Was she still mad that I had been late? Was she still fuming about the dirty dishrag smell that floated like a rank cloud out of the back shed, into the passageway, right through the screen door, and into the café? Or was she still afraid that Dad would weasel his way back into our lives?

I hoped it was the dirty dishrag smell, because I didn't want to see Dad ever again.

Becoming the father

WHEN I RECENTLY READ *memoir writer Vivian Gornick's observation that "We become what is done to us," I started to understand why I behave the way I do.*

After my father was long gone from our lives, I found myself repeating his loathsome habits: not just pocketing a few quarters because I had seen him steal a paint brush, but shaming people I didn't know, erupting toward those who slighted me to protect myself, jokingly making insults masquerading as flattery—all the bad behaviors I'd learned from him years before.

After my account of the beating I took at the hand of my father at the diner, you might wonder why his physically abusive behavior doesn't show up earlier in the memoir. I'll admit, up until now, I've been afraid to look deeper—only willing to describe how his habits of neglect, self-centeredness, and off-color humor might prove that abuse comes in many forms.

As a young adult, I started to be convinced that my own bad behaviors were triggered by my father's wretched habits. Is it possible that, as a child, I feared his eruptions at times yet at others craved his attention and approval, because I had buried the physical abuses and only remembered the joking, the clowning, the happy-go-lucky personality he used to disguise his aggression? And was this the reason I was willing to go into the shed to find the basketball, knowing deep down inside that something painful was about to happen?

Many years later, what jarred me into remembering that beating was hearing my sister tell my wife, "Daddy used to beat the holy shit out of Joey. And Dad got angrier and even more crazy when Joey wouldn't stop crying." The revelation was terrifying. But it forced me to look deeper into my past to uncover more conscious knowledge of that particular beating. That's when I started to faintly recognize that there must have been other occurrences—perhaps too painful to remember.

This memoir—and my need to construct a narrative of events I wasn't sure about—has helped me realize that a coping mechanism surely must have been necessary back then. And the major device I used must have been my mother's food—a major prop in the drama. Such comforting objects have helped me to understand that every distraction—every bit of intense concentration I used to assuage the bitter moments and recraft a safe story—helped to soothe the underlying traumas.

This posed yet another important question: where did my consciousness go to hide during those rough and tumble experiences?

My belief is that fantasy is the province of the abused child. And that fantasy turns into an elaborate fiction, first of all, in diverting one's mind from the painful experiences, and secondly, in constructing a narrative that would help me recall a verifiable memory of the events. And this coping mechanism must have worked, because years later, when I told Laura I fabricated many of the connecting stories to make sense out of the chaos, she said, "No, Joey, you didn't make that up—that's how it happened."

This is what I've come to believe has occurred: In the first instance of coping with the abuse, I forced myself to turn toward any distraction that could create a mental escape route—often the closest thing at hand: the food, the music, the fantasy of cowgirls on the bedroom wall, the patterns of design and color in the draperies and fabric of our lives. These surface textures became my salvation—helping me to camouflage the pain in a creative patina. As I've said before, I believe that this is where art is born. But now my understanding goes even further: My need for emotional (artistic) expression has helped me turn my fantasies into fictions in trying to reconstruct a story from my memory of those events I allowed myself to remember. I now call it "placing together pieces of the puzzle so I can get a picture."

In trying to remember the abuses, I've forced myself to make sense out of hazy remembrances by reconstructing a story with fabricated facts and situations (or those lifted from other, related, yet less damaging events), so I didn't have to remember the sordid details of the original experiences. By linking known events with repressed ones, I've been able to attain a glimmer of understanding and make sense out of them.

But before I was able to re-experience and write about the painful events, I had to be willing to go deep enough to describe them truthfully. I'm told that this takes courage, and that those of us who survive have done so through the spiritual journey of understanding that "something was going on." This knowledge didn't make the process any easier.

Until I tackled this memoir, I had been circling around the experience. Explaining, justifying. But to make the experiences dramatic (for the reader) and therapeutic (for myself), I knew I had to venture into what I still call "going into the dark room," into the ominous cave of the unknown to tell my secrets.

Secrets which, up until now, before detailing the incident of abuse behind the cafe, I've not only refused to tell others but refused to tell myself.

Chapter Seventeen:
Manny Perez and the Milk Football

MANNY PEREZ WAS FRIENDLY, outgoing, and dependable most of the time. When he started working at the drive-in dairy on Avalon Boulevard, he offered to buy me, at his cost, the newest thing in milk packaging. The milk was in a cardboard container that weighed about twenty-five pounds and, although it was awkward to carry, you didn't have to pick it up to pour it. You just sat it on a shelf in the fridge, popped a plastic spout out of a cardboard box and poured the milk from there.

It cost me lots more than my mother and I had ever spent for milk—around two dollars and change for three gallons. Until then we had only bought milk a quart at a time, or on occasion we'd pay 49 cents for a half-gallon at Von's. This time Mom agreed to give me the money because Manny was so nice to do it for us, and she rarely refused anything that I thought was a good idea.

For some reason Manny didn't show up with the milk after dinner like he promised. He didn't show up later either. I did a little homework, but I couldn't concentrate. I listened to the last few innings of the Dodgers game, but all I could think about was Manny and the milk. It got later and later. And after having spent that kind of money, I finally decided, well maybe that's a lot of milk to buy all at once.

The more I thought about it, the more I started to feel glad that Manny hadn't shown up; and I hoped he had forgotten the deal. Maybe the next day I could tell him, Let's just forget it. Mom and I can buy our milk at the store a half-gallon at a time like we always did.

I went to bed early, hoping I would fall asleep, forget all about Manny and the milk and wake up the next day without having caused a lot of commotion in the house in the middle of the night. But as I was falling off to sleep, I heard a scratching at the window. At first I thought it was a bug caught in the screen or some kind of bird tapping. But when the scratching got louder and the pattern more regular, I realized it was Manny.

I tried to make believe I was asleep. Maybe he would go away, I thought. If he had brought the milk, maybe he would take it home with him, put in in his refrigerator and wake up his mom instead of mine.

But no. Manny was persistent. Even if it meant scoring a goal for the other team.

That night was no different. He wasn't the kind of kid to be defeated by a dark house or a closed window. Before too long, I heard the window slide open.

"Hey, Joe," he whispered through the half-opened window, "You awake?"

I kept my eyes shut tight and didn't move. I wanted him to leave. Instead Manny opened the window the rest of the way, and I sank deeper under the covers. He scooted the milk container through the window and onto my desk, and he boosted himself up and started climbing in.

"What's going on?" I said. "Who is it?"

"Don't worry," he said, "It's Manny and I've got your milk."

By then I realized I had to get up.

There we were, whispering to one another in the dim light of my room, exchanging the milk for the few dollars I had wadded up and stashed into the coin pocket of my dungarees, which were bunched up on top of my sneakers in the corner. Manny stood there counting the money while I stood in my socks and underwear, holding a milk container the size of a rugby ball that I had already decided was too much for a twelve-year-old kid to drink before it went bad.

When Manny slipped back out the window, I had to put the milk in the fridge and, of course, you know who woke up and followed me into the kitchen,

"Joey," Mom said, "What's going on out here? What's all the noise?"

There really wasn't that much noise, just me opening the refrigerator and sliding the milk onto the shelf. But Mom could hear anything. Like Dad used to say, "Ya can't put anything ova on ya Mutha, Joey. She can hear a mouse fart a mile away."

"It's me, Mom," I whispered, "Manny just dropped off the milk and I'm putting it away. Go back to sleep."

"Manny and the milk?" she said. "I didn't hear the door open."

"Well, he came in through the window, Mom."

"Bringing milk in through the window?" she said, starting to wake up. I could imagine her in a few minutes biting her finger and getting worked up. But now she was still whispering. I felt us both hunching over, trying to make ourselves small and inconspicuous as we spoke. It was something I'd learned from her, as if when whispering you also had to hunker down so you could hide from anyone who might be looking or listening to what you were talking about.

"I don't understand that Manny," she said. "What's he think he's doing waking people up in the middle of the night, bringing milk through the bedroom window?"

"Well, he's gone now," I said. "So let's go back to sleep.

175

At least the milk's here and tomorrow we can start to drink it."

"I still don't know what we're going to do with all that milk," she said, scratching her head, turning out the light, and shuffling back to bed. I was starting to feel guilty about the milk again when she stopped and turned around. "Joey," she said. "Sit down."

Oh no, I thought. She's going to tell me something. No, Mom, I wanted to say, Do we have to talk now? Can't we just start drinking the milk tomorrow and forget about it? I'm sorry, I'm sorry.

I was already beginning to hate the milk. I hated Manny for being such an optimist. I swore I'd do my best to drink the milk before it spoiled to convince Mom that her faith in agreeing to buy it wasn't a mistake. That would be my penance. I would drink more milk than I ever had since I was a little kid. Even if it took two weeks to finish. Even if I got sick. Even if, as usual, I would want to shout to myself, *I don't care anymore. The milk can go bad and I don't care if Mom thinks I'm an idiot for wasting her money.*

Please, Mom, I thought, *Let's not talk.*

"It always seems best to do things for others in life," my mother said, as she settled into a chair at the kitchen table. She didn't bother turning on the light, since the streetlamp on the corner was shining in. "We always wonder what others might think about us or how they might judge us for our actions. But deep down we're afraid of how we see ourselves."

At first it seemed like she was talking about Manny. But I could tell she was leading up to something else.

"Remember the two men that came into the café with Bill?" she said. I knew what she was leading up to, now. I didn't want to hear it.

I was beginning to feel the same discomfiting feeling I had

176

when Manny didn't show up with the milk. I didn't want to talk about it. If it wasn't going to be about the milk or about Manny, it must be about Dad.

"I had to tell your father to leave," Mom said. "I had to." The minute she said it, I knew it was going to get a lot more awkward than that. But all she said was, "He's in Reno now."

"Ma?"

"The two guys talking to Bill were looking for Dad. But Bill covered for your father; they knew one another from before. He didn't tell them anything about Reno.

"Oh well," Ma said. "Reno's farther away, so maybe we won't see him so much."

Somehow I thought she was hiding something. But I guess we were meant to leave it at that. It took a long time for us to finish all that milk. Just like a bad memory, it lingered on until we had to pour the final few drops down the drain. The box, even when crushed up, took up a painfully disturbing amount of space in the garbage.

MOM'S CONFESSION ABOUT DAD being gone settled my mind in a liberating way that I'd never felt before.

After we lived without milk for a long while, I started craving it again, so we went back to buying it a small container at a time. A few weeks later Mom sent me to the store for a single half gallon. I remember feeling free because Dad was further away, feeling as if I could run a hundred miles an hour. So, I started to run. I gathered up speed. In the brown sack, moist from the container, the milk felt like a football, so I tucked it under my arm and zigzagged back and forth, giving straight arms to the front and side of me, avoiding imaginary tacklers and hurling myself into the air. I ran along the paths we kids had beaten through the green sticker bushes, freshly up in spring. All out through the oil fields near our house and over the railroad track,

I sprinted toward home and a touchdown. In the last few yards before our street, my foot hit a ditch; I hesitated, lost my grip, and fumbled. The milk football squirted up and out of reach in front of me. It paused there for a moment, suspended. I felt the milk gods and muses that haunt mischievous young boys frowning down on me when the milk container landed right under my footfall, where I couldn't help but stomp it. I came down in a crash and my foot flattened the container with the full weight of my body and it sent me sprawling into the dirt. I started to cry even before I could pick myself up. My tears were not caused so much by the fall but by the mortification of having wasted food and the pang of having to tell my mother I had turned the milk to mud for the sake of an imaginary touchdown.

What would she say? I was always gambling with my responsibility. When I arrived home, crying and muddy, my mother held on to me and soothed my pain by telling me she didn't care about the milk. She just wanted to know whether I was all right. I was confused. My own suffering had seemed so real. I almost craved for it to be recognized. Instead, we talked a little about the silly container of milk we had bought from Manny.

We sat in the kitchen. By then it was just Mom and me, because Laura had moved out of the house and gone to work in Long Beach. Mom pulled out some crumb cake she had bought at the supermarket. It was in one of those cellophane wrappers and she said it was lousy, because it wasn't fresh. But it was all we had. "They don't have any decent bakeries out here," she said. Since there wasn't any milk in the house, we both washed down the crumb cake with some cold coffee left over from the morning.

That night when Mom spoke to me after Manny dropped off the milk, I was strongly anticipating what she was trying to tell me, and what it might have to do with Dad. The questions kept popping up, but I didn't want to know the answers. What did my guilt about Manny and the milk have to do with the hollow feeling I got when I was five years old, and Dad would put his hand on his belt and immediately, I would stop, cower, and run to Mom? All these thoughts raced through my mind as protection from what Mom was going to say now. When she finally got it out, it was a thousand times worse than what I had imagined.

First, she started to cry. She became short of breath. She couldn't get a single word out. When I started to cry in reaction to her sobbing, she pulled herself together.

"Joey, those men from the café," Mom said. "They came two weeks later to tell me Daddy died."

And the tears came gushing down again.

"Daddy's dead, and I didn't know how to tell you," she said. "It's so sad. It's so sad."

I didn't know how to react, and my own crying became even more intense. I couldn't understand why she was sobbing. Did she still love him after everything he had done? I thought we were supposed to be glad he was finally out of our lives after all the misery he had caused. I thought we were supposed to hate him.

And I was finally willing to admit it to myself.

We sat there at the kitchen table with the streetlamp shining in, weeping and holding one another, rocking back and forth. It was then that the hunkering down in the darkness and the whispering finally became the protection we needed from anyone else being able to see or feel our grief.

Then Mom explained to me why she cried so hard when she told me about Dad. She confessed that she couldn't bear to see its effects on me. She knew I would take it hard. She said we weren't supposed to hate Dad for what he'd done to us. And that I wasn't supposed to hate him for all the misery he had caused her, that that was between them. She said she just got to the point where she couldn't live with him and that sometimes things happen to let you know you have to go on alone.

I asked Mom if it was like Dad had always said: "Sometimes you gotta do something to change your luck." But Mom said, "It doesn't have anything to do with luck, Joseph."

Whenever she called me Joseph I knew it was the truth.

Then she told me everything would be all right. But I'm not sure it changed the way I felt about Dad. Hate might be a strong word for it. But some of the pain had finally been relieved if only by a little—especially knowing we'd never see him again.

The art of deflection

I'VE LEARNED ONLY IN THE PAST FEW YEARS that I indulge in the art of deflecting a conversation away from a topic that I would rather not discuss. Early therapy taught me that it's best to come clean about one's life, to express oneself—talk about what people might ask. But more recently, I've learned that the fear of being truthful often can cause me to veer away from the uncomfortable emotional place where an honest revelation might lead. And what people might mistake about it. And think badly of me for it. I found it easier to insert a diversionary anecdote, description, or joke into a conversation in response to a question that might lead to an embarrassing admission. Where on earth could I have learned this tactic? My mother did not possess this art of shifting a conversation into another direction. No, it was my father who was a master of what I now call the "fabricated segue"—the idle chit-chat, which takes a detour toward another topic of conversation. Assuredly, I learned it from him. Not by tutelage but by observing how he behaved.

I'm hoping that other such revelations will show themselves to me in the years to come, now that I've been able to complete this book and move on to other, equally fruitful projects. As they say in theater and other pursuits: "fingers crossed."

Chapter Eighteen:
The Small Dark Man in the Corner

MOST PEOPLE WHO KNEW MY FATHER believe that it was his life-style—all the smoking, drinking, and gambling—that struck him down with a massive heart attack on a street in Reno, Nevada, in 1961. But I'll always believe that, as usual, he was feeling a little preoccupied with himself and carefree that day, and on the way to his favorite casino, he walked around a corner and ran into—who else but Freddie the bookie.

It's just my guess that seeing Freddie face-to-face after all those years of hiding and running simply caused Dad to die of fright.

In those first few years after he was gone, while Mom was working hard to keep food on the table, I learned to cook for myself. I went from eating toast and coffee for breakfast to making myself bacon and eggs. Having picked up some tips from Mom and from working at the café, I honed my skills in the kitchen. I learned to make lemon meringue pie on my own, without my mother's help or my father telling me that boys don't make desserts.

Around that time I remember hearing an interview on the radio in which a Buddhist monk from India was stressing the importance of concentrating on whatever you're doing. "To concentrate precisely on what you are doing," he said, "that is yoga."

The monk made his point somewhat crudely—and that's what made me think of Dad—when he said: "Even when you go to the bathroom, you must concentrate on what you are doing. That is the highest form of yoga."

So my father—all those times back in Queens when he sat on the can—must have been meditating. Right. And I suppose, to make his meditation even more intense, he had five experiences going on at once. It's not hard to imagine his mind darting back and forth from the Dodger box score to a puff of a Camel cigarette, to a bite of chicharrones, and finally to a gulp of beer; it was the same way he carried on in his everyday life. No one will ever know what degree of importance he gave to the actual reason he had gone there to sit. It must have been essential to the ritual, for he sat there so long and so often that we all began to believe that to him it was a natural place to be—as natural as crawling through the jungles of Puerto Rico and a lot less risky than squatting in the alley behind the shoe shop playing dice.

SOMETIMES I THINK HE'S STILL OUT THERE. Still hiding. Still running. Since I never actually saw him buried, sometimes I ask myself, "What if he's still alive?"

I often think I see him in a crowd somewhere. Sometimes in Europe, or when I'm in New York City or at the County Fair, or when I take my godchildren to the beach or boardwalk, there's a small, dark man leaning against a wall, in a hidden corner, smoking a cigarette. It seems as though he might still be trying to figure out a scheme that would help him make amends for all those things he did to Federico. To my Mom. To Laura and me. And maybe he would tell us that it's all right now, that he was sorry. And then maybe I could tell him I was sorry, too, and that so much time has passed and, because he has been such a memory for so long, that I'm not sure whether any of it really happened. Or if it did, it didn't matter. Or maybe I have learned to forgive him.

Then maybe I could invite him home and introduce him to my wife, Gayle. And we all could sit down and drink beer together. And perhaps share a meal. Maybe I could make him a plate of pasta or a bowl of pastina. Or . . . I know . . . arroz con pollo.

So many times, when I thought I saw him at the boardwalk or at the beach, I wanted to run over and say, "Want a hot dog, Daddy?" Or "Want an ice cream cone?" But I'd get distracted by the crowd, by the amusements, or by the kids wanting to go on a ride.

Then I'd look over to the corner by the wall and the small dark man would be gone.

The Recipes

Minestra de Verdura
Broccoli Rabe and Garlic Soup

Serves two to four

PERHAPS MY FIRST FOOD MEMORY—besides pastina—is of this
rich, murky, sweetly-bitter soup my Aunt Mary loved. And,
made with enough pepper flakes, a dish that made Dad enjoy
it too.

Aunt Mary was the saint of the family and the maker of great
soup. After you taste this rich, amber-green broth you'll know
why it represents our bittersweet life in Queens. I'm not sure if
Mom used the pepper flakes, but she once accused some un-
mentionable someone of "waltzing into the kitchen" and taking
it upon themself to spice it up with a healthy sprinkle or two.

> 1 bunch of broccoli rabe, washed and trimmed
>   of half an inch of its bottom stem, cut into
>   one-inch pieces
> 1 medium yellow onion, peeled and sliced thin
> 6 to 8 cloves of garlic, smashed with the side of
>   the knife, peeled and rough chopped
> ½ teaspoon pepper flakes
> 2 teaspoons kosher salt
> Freshly ground pepper to taste
> 1 14-ounce can chicken broth (2 cups)
> 2 to 3 cups water
> grated Parmesan cheese for garnish
>   and a drizzle of olive oil

* * * *

IN A MEDIUM CASSEROLE, place the olive oil, garlic, and onion, and sauté over low heat four to five minutes, until the aromatics are limp but not burnt. Add the pepper flakes.

Add the broccoli rabe (it's okay if it's still a little wet) and the salt and pepper and toss with the oil several minutes just to coat and cook it a little.

Add the stock and water and turn up the heat. When the soup starts to boil, reduce the heat to low and let simmer for 20 minutes, until the greens get almost "mushy." It's the peasant way! Like Freddie the bookie used to say, "Trust me on this one," and he knew a little about soup, too.

When it's done, correct for salt, ladle into soup bowls, garnish with the grated Parmesan and a light drizzle of olive oil.

If you want to add another peasant touch, toast a piece of French bread to make a crostino and place it in the bowl before you ladle the soup on top.

And *mangia!*

Pastina

Serves 4 to 6

THIS IS THE SOUP that caused me to dig deep to discover why Dad had to leave Queens to escape Freddie's clutches. Whenever I see it on a restaurant menu, it makes me think about how I got my head stuck in the wrought iron security bars of our kitchen window. You don't have to go through all that anguish to enjoy it. Just the same, it can soothe any uncomfortable experience.

> 1 whole chicken, cut into pieces
> 10 to 12 cups water, enough to cover chicken
> 1 carrot, peeled and cut up
> 2 medium onions, quartered
> 2 stalks celery
> 2 small handfuls of pastina, star-shaped pasta
>   (1/3 cup)
> ¼ cup fresh parsley, chopped fine
> A little grated Parmesan cheese to sprinkle on top

PLACE THE CHICKEN in a large stock pot and cover with the water and all the vegetables.

Bring the water to a boil, then turn down the heat and simmer for two hours.

Turn the heat off and strain the broth into a smaller pot. Discard the vegetables and, when the chicken is cool, strip it off the bones and save it for chicken cacciatore.

Let the broth cool, then stick the pot in the fridge overnight to chill. The next day, skim off the fat from the top of the broth and discard. (You should end up with 5 to 6 cups of broth before reducing.) Reheat the broth and cook it slowly over medium heat to reduce it by about one quarter ("Don't boil it too hard," Freddie said, "or you'll bruise da broth.")

Pour in a handful or two of pastina macaroni (don't use too much, 'cause it swells up when it cooks.).

Simmer about 10 minutes until the pasta is done to your liking. Ladle it into bowls, then add the parsley and serve with a little grated Parmesan on top.

Mom's Tomato Sauce
Gravy, the Real Stuff

Serves 4 to 6

NEVER MIND that you cook this stuff for days. And never mind that I got most of the ideas from Aunt Margie. Mom's must have been similar. Anyway, the meat is optional. Use it only if you've got it; we rarely did. The canned tomato paste in the recipe, of course, would be considered a sin from Freddie the Bookie's point-of-view. His mom made her own u'stratto (I wish I had a recipe), since she was Sicilian.

For the tomatoes, you can used canned or the simple tomato sauce on page 192, run through a food mill to take out the lumps.

> ¼ cup olive oil
> 6 cloves of garlic, minced
> 1 medium carrot, peeled and minced fine
> 1 stalk of celery, minced fine
> ½ cup minced finocchio bulb (they call it fennel these days. It went out of favor for a while, but it's back.)
> 1 small can tomato paste
> 1 small (½ pound) skirt steak, chopped fine
> 1/2 cup red wine
> 8 cups tomatoes, scalded, skinned, seeded, and passed through a food mill
> (or canned plum tomatoes diced finely)
> 3 teaspoons salt
> 1 1/2 teaspoons freshly ground pepper
> 1 Tablespoon sugar
> 1 teaspoon cinnamon

* * * *

IN A LARGE, HEAVY STOCK POT, heat the oil. Add the garlic, carrot, celery, onion, and fennel. Sauté 8 to 10 minutes over medium-high heat, until the mixture becomes lightly browned. Add the meat and keep stirring. Don't leave it alone. Stay there and stir until the meat is just brown. Deglaze the pan with the red wine and stir for several minutes.

Add the tomato paste and stir to combine with the flame on low to medium. Cook the mixture 4 to 5 minutes. Add the tomatoes, salt, pepper, and cinnamon. Stir it all together.

Cook the sauce over very low heat (maybe even with a trivet), 5 to 6 hours, adding water as necessary if it starts to get thick, which it will. Some mothers cook this overnight. My mom never did. She thought she might burn down the house, or worse, burn the gravy!

Mom's Simple Red Sauce

Makes 2 cups

8 to 10 medium Italian plum tomatoes
2 Tablespoons pureed or chopped garlic
4 to 5 anchovy filets, mashed
1 sprig fresh parsley (2 Tablespoons chopped)
1/4 cup olive oil

SET A POT OF WATER over high heat. When it comes to a boil, gently drop in the tomatoes for 2 to 4 minutes, until the skins blister. Remove from the water with a slotted spoon and set aside to cool. Slice the tomatoes in half and gently squeeze out the seeds and remove the skins. Crush the tomatoes with your hands into 1-inch pieces. And set aside.

In a medium-sized saucepan, cook the olive oil, garlic, and anchovies over medium low heat until lightly browned (about 4 to 5 minutes). Gradually ladle in half of the tomatoes and stir another few minutes to make a dark puree. Add the rest of the crushed tomatoes and cook 20 to 30 minutes on low heat. Add the parsley and correct for salt and pepper. The sauce can be cooled before using or used directly while still warm.

Balsamic Cherry Tomatoes

1 basket cherry tomatoes
3 cloves garlic, minced
2 Tablespoons Balsamic Vinegar
2 Tablespoons extra virgin olive oil
Salt and pepper to taste
2 Tablespoons minced basil or parsley, as garnish

Preheat oven to 350 degrees

PUT THE TOMATOES in a roasting pan just large enough to hold them in one layer. Drizzle the balsamic and olive oil and sprinkle the garlic on top along with the salt and pepper.

Roast at 350 for 10 minutes. Toss the mixture to incorporate and to mash the tomatoes a bit.

Roast another 8 to 10 minutes, until tomatoes are soft. Add the parsley and/or basil.

Melanzane alla Parmigiana

Serves 4

I ALWAYS WONDERED why they call it Eggplant Parmesan if there's no Parmesan cheese in most recipes. (Could it have originated in Parma?) Somehow adding Parmesan was the old wives' tale Mom spoke about, and rumor was that some mothers added the grated cheese to a bit of flour for dredging the slices if they were too moist for frying. I add the cheese here, but it's optional.

Preheat oven to 400 degrees

1 medium eggplant, sliced lengthwise,
    1/4 inch thick (or just a bit thicker)
1 1/2 Tablespoons salt
1 cup all-purpose flour
1/2 cup toasted breadcrumbs
1/3 cup grated Parmesan cheese
1/2 cup olive oil for frying (or combo of
    avocado oil and olive oil)
1 ½ to 2 cups of your favorite marinara sauce
6 to 8 ounces mozzarella cheese, sliced 1/8" thick
2 large eggs whisked with 2 Tablespoons water

PLACE THE EGGPLANT SLICES in a colander or on a baking sheet lined with paper towels. Sprinkle both sides of the slices with the salt. Let drain 30 minutes to 1 hour. Pat the slices dry with paper towels. In a medium oval plate, mix the flour, the bread crumbs, and the Parmesan cheese. Whisk the egg and water and first dip each slice in the egg mixture, then dredge each slice in the flour and breadcrumb mixture to coat before frying.

Fry the slices in batches, using a little of the olive oil for each batch, until crisp and golden.

Drain on paper towels. In a 7-inch by 10-inch baking dish, place about 1/4 of the sauce on the bottom. Then start layering eggplant slices, more sauce, a layer of cheese, and continue until all ingredients are gone and there's some sauce and one layer of mozzarella on top.

Bake the casserole 25 to 30 minutes until the top becomes rich and bubbly. Allow to cool 10 minutes before slicing and serving.

Chicken *Cacciatore*

Serves 4 to 6

THIS IS THE EASY VERSION. You can jazz it up by sautéing extra diced bell pepper, diced green olives, and onions in a bit of olive oil and Balsamic vinegar, adding the red sauce and chicken and warming it before serving. But Mom liked to keep it simple.

> 3 Tablespoons olive oil
> 1/2 medium yellow onion, julienned (1/2 cup)
> 1 green bell pepper, cut in small julienne
> 3 Tablespoons pitted green olives
> 4 cups gravy (what most of the world calls
>   tomato sauce), your favorite simple recipe
> 1/2 chicken (from Pastina recipe) having
>   been boiled, cooled, and stripped
>   from the bones and shredded
> grated Parmesan and minced parsley
>   to taste, as garnish.

IN A SMALL SAUCE PAN, heat the olive oil and sauté the onion briefly. Add the bell pepper and olives and sauté another 4 to 5 minutes. Add the tomato sauce and heat just until bubbly. Place the warmed shredded chicken in the sauce pan and warm over medium heat a few minutes. Serve immediately as a side dish or over cooked spaghetti, garnished with the grated Parmesan and parsley.

Aglio e Olio
Pasta in Garlic and Olive Oil

Serves Two:
Me and Mom because Dad didn't like it and
Laura was always out singing *a capella* on the block

DR. BOCCARDI ALWAYS PRESCRIBED this whenever I had been eating
aspirin. Or when I had any kind of compromised digestion. Which
I often did. It's good for "agita" as long as you leave out the pepper
flakes and don't use too much garlic.

- 3 Tablespoons extra virgin olive oil
- 3 to 4 cloves garlic, minced
- 6 ounces spaghetti (just enough that you can hold
    wrapped between your thumb and fingers
    real tight)
- ½ teaspoon red pepper flakes (optional)
- 2 Tablespoons chopped parsley
- 3 to 4 Tablespoons grated Parmesan cheese

HEAT THE OIL in a skillet over medium heat. Add the minced garlic
and cook until just golden. Turn off the heat.

Cook the pasta in a medium saucepan of salted, boiling water
until al dente. When the pasta is ready, scoop it out with a large
fork and add it to the garlic and oil mixture. Then turn up the heat
to medium.

Add about ½ cup of the pasta water to the pan and cook while
stirring constantly until the water has all evaporated and the pasta
is cooked to your liking.

Add half of the parsley and all of the pepper flakes if you're using
them.

Remove to pasta bowls and sprinkle with the rest of the parsley
and a little of the grated Parmesan cheese.

Braciola—Stuffed Skirt Steak

Serves 4
Preheat oven to 350 degrees

THIS RECIPE IS LINKED to the time Dad fixed the knife cut on Eddie Ryan's shoes by gluing ground shoe leather into the crack, then—according to my Uncle Johnny—grinding it down so "the naked eye couldn't tell da difference." It was the same night we caught Johnny bragging about his secret technique for adding the egg. But now I'm realizing no one uses egg at all, it was just Johnny's penchant for fictional elaboration (read "lying") in telling a story.

> 1 skirt steak weighing 1 1/2 pounds
> Salt and pepper to taste
> 5 to 6 slices of Prosciutto
> ½ cup chopped spinach
> ½ cup chopped parsley
> 6 cloves garlic, minced fine
> 3/4 cup breadcrumbs
> 1 ½ cup grated Parmesan
> 2 Tablespoons olive oil and 2 Tablespoons butter
> 2 (28-ounce) cans Italian plum tomatoes
>> (To prep the tomatoes, sauté 6 cloves of garlic, minced, in a few tablespoons of olive oil, add the tomatoes and simmer with a little water for a few hours over low heat, stirring occasionally.)

PLACE THE STEAK between 2 pieces of wax paper and pound until it's about ¼-inch thick (thin as possible). The steak should measure about 6 to 7 inches wide by 20 inches long. Set aside.

Poach the spinach in a little pan of hot water over low to medium heat for a few minutes. When cool, squeeze it dry with your hands.

Heat the butter in a skillet and sauté the garlic until translucent. Let cool.

In a medium bowl, combine the breadcrumbs, grated Parmesan, parsley, and spinach, until well blended.

Lay the steak out on a flat surface, fat side down, and cover the meat with the prosciutto slices, then about a ¾-inch-thick layer of the filling.

The mixture should be an inch or so from the back edge, and then roll it into a log of about 2 inches in diameter.

Secure with toothpicks (tying with kitchen twine is best). Heat the olive oil and butter in a casserole pan large enough to hold the log (or cut in 8-inch lengths to accommodate) and fry the meat until brown on all sides (4 to 5 minutes).

Pour 4 to 6 cups of the tomato sauce over the meat and bake in the 350-degree oven for 1 hour 30 minutes.

Let the logs cool ten minutes, then slice and serve with some of the sauce on top.

Pasta e Fagioli
Pasta and Bean Soup

6 to 8 servings

EVERYBODY'S MOM made this (if they were Italian). Every version was different. Every kid said his mom's was best. The only one we never argued with was Freddie, who told us you had to de-gas the beans and he was right. Besides, you pretty much listened to whatever Freddie said.

> One 15-ounce can cooked Cannellini beans
>   (great northern, or white), or if using dried,
>   be sure to follow Freddie's instructions for
>   degasing or he'll turn over in his grave
> ¼ cup olive oil
> 2 medium carrots, diced
> 2 stalks celery, diced fine
> 1 medium yellow onion, diced
> 4 cloves garlic, minced
> 1 15-ounce can peeled plum tomatoes, or if fresh,
>   scalded, skinned, seeded, and pureed (2 cups)
> 1 ½ to 2 teaspoons minced herbs (oregano, sage,
>   rosemary)
> 1 to ½ cup dried pasta (Tubetti, Tubettini, or Ditalini)
> 3 to 4 cups chicken stock (or water)
> 1 piece of leftover Parmesan rind
> Salt and pepper, to taste
> grated Parmesan cheese for sprinkling as garnish
> olive oil for drizzling

*   *   *   *

IF YOU'RE USING DRIED BEANS, put them in a pot and cover with water by 3 or 4 inches. Bring to a boil. Turn off the heat and let the beans rest for at least a couple hours (or overnight). Drain the beans and cover with fresh water. Cook the beans 1 ½ to 2 hours until tender, adding a little salt and pepper. Whether you're using canned or cooked beans, puree half of the bean mixture using a food mill or immersion blender and set aside.

Heat the olive oil in a skillet and sauté the carrots, celery, garlic, and onions until deep, rich, and aromatic. Add the tomatoes, salt, and pepper. Sauté 5 to 8 minutes, stirring constantly.

If you're using homemade chicken stock, reduce it down from 8 cups to 4. "Don't bruise the broth," as Freddie used to say, by boiling it on too high a flame.

Add the beans, herbs, Parmesan rind, and the macaroni to the pot containing the tomato-vegetable mixture. Cook over low heat for 15 to 20 minutes until the pasta is cooked and all the flavors meld together. Remove the Parmesan rin and discard. Adjust salt and pepper.

Serve in soup bowls with a drizzle of olive oil and a little grated Parmesan on top.

Mom's Ricotta Ravioli

4 to 6 servings
Half recipe makes 18 to 24 ravioli

LIKE MOM DID, it's best for you to let these "Ravis" rest on a big bed covered with a big white sheet after they're finished. It's important for them to dry out properly so they don't get mushy and break apart in the boiling water. I tried rolling out the dough by hand, the old fashioned way, with a wooden rolling pin. But you can't get it thin enough without years of practice. So I recommend using a pasta machine, either hand-cranked or electric. My favorite is the Kitchen Aid mixer fitted with the pasta roller attachement.

Dough ingredients:	Half Recipe
4 1/2 cups all-purpose flour (or 00)	2 1/4 cups
6 eggs	3 eggs
2 Tablspoons milk	3 tsp

Filling ingredients:	
3 cups ricotta cheese	1 1/2 cups
1 egg, beaten	1/2 egg
1/2 to 1 teaspoon each, salt and pepper	1/4 tsp. ea.
½ cup chopped parsley	1/4 cup
3 cups grated Parmesan cheese	1 1/2 cups
2 teaspoons ground nutmeg	1 tsp

The sauce:
6 cups of your favorite Marinara sauce

PLACE THE FLOUR IN A MOUND on your worktable, make a well inside and add the eggs and milk.

With your fingers, scramble the eggs and start combining in some of the flour. When the flour is nearly all incorporated, use both hands to combine the rest of the flour, and knead the dough 5 or 6 minutes, until smooth and satiny. Don't over mix the dough or it will get like a rubber band, Mom said.

Let the dough rest, covered with a damp towel, for 30 to 40 minutes. Keep it hidden from hungry teenagers who might want to tear off a piece and eat it.

For the filling:

IN A MEDIUM BOWL, add the ricotta and the beaten egg and mix with a spatula until well blended. Add the grated Parmesan and mix to combine. The filling should be just dry enough to hold together on a spoon, like small-curd cottage cheese.

If the mixture is too wet, add an extra few tablespoons of the Parmesan. Add only the amount you think you'll need. Better a little too dry than too wet or it will seep through the dough.

Place the filling into the fridge for 20 minutes to firm it up.

For rolling out the dough:

1) Dust the dough lightly with flour.

2) To start with, use the thickest setting on the pasta rolling machine. Cut the dough in quarters and, working with each piece individually, pass the dough through the rollers; then fold over and repeat the process, rolling and folding at least 4 or 5 times, until the dough is smooth with no rough edges.

3) Gradually reduce the thickness setting, each time passing the dough through the rollers until it measures 5 inches by about 12 to 14 inches long.

4) Roll the dough as thin as possible without tearing it. I always use the next-to-last setting on the machine, which seems thin enough. The resulting thin dough will help make the edges more tender after cooking.

5) Roll out the second of the four pieces of dough the

same as the first; this will be the top. NOTE: After you've filled these two pieces and made the ravioli, do the same with the remaining two quarters of dough.

To fill the Ravioli:

1) Place both pieces of dough on your work table with a fine dusting of flour. In the bowl, divide the filling amount in half so you know how much to use for these two pieces. Use a teaspoon to place walnut-sized dollops of the filling, in two rows, an inch or so apart across the length of one of the dough pieces. You should get 6 to 7 rows of two or about 12 to 14 ravioli.

2) Place the second sheet over the filling dollops, creating a strip of dough with lumps. Use the edge of your hand to press channels between each lump of filling.

3) With a zigzag rolling wheel, cut each ravioli into 2" squares. Then prick each one with a fork to make sure they don't bloat up when boiled.

Repeat the roll-out and filling process with the remaining 2 pieces of dough and remaining filling.

WHEN THE RAVIS ARE ALL FILLED, place them on baking trays lined with semolina- or flour-dusted towels. Let the Ravis dry for 30 or 40 minutes and turn them over midway to make sure they're not sticking. Then, if you prefer, place them on plates in the fridge.

To cook, bring a large pot of salted water to a boil. Gently drop in half a dozen ravis at a time. After 6 to 8 minutes and they've floated to the top, scoop one out of the water with a slotted spoon and test the edges for doneness (delicate to the bite). If the edge isn't done to your liking, give that batch another few minutes of cooking. Cook the rest of the batch as above.

Place two or three ravis on a plate and cover with your favorite heated marinara sauce, a sprinkle of Parmesan, and *Mangia!*

Cream

Serves 4
Laura, Rosemarie, Ant'ny, and Me

WHEN WE GOT BACK from the Cisco and Pancho appearance at the Silvercup, Aunt Rose and cousins Rosemarie and Anthony were at the house. Even though Mom didn't notice anything, Aunt Rose saw that I needed a treat. She always made this pudding to soothe our ills. Although I mentioned earlier that Aunt Rose used cornstarch, milk, and no eggs, I since discovered that this peasant slurry is made with thickened egg yolks, milk, and sugar. You can serve it warm in bowls, refrigerated in cups (it gets a nice skin on top), or mixed with whipped cream to fill cream puffs.

> 2 cups whole milk (or half and half)
> 5 egg yolks (at room temperature)
> 1/2 cup sugar (scant)
> 1/2 teaspoon vanilla extract
> Cinnamon to taste

IN A SMALL CASSEROLE or saucepan, heat the milk until it's just warm.

Separate the yolks and place them in a medium-sized bowl and beat with a wire whisk. Add the sugar and combine fully. Pour a few tablespoons of the warmed milk into the bowl with the yolks and mix to combine and get the eggs to the right temperature.

Slowly add the warm milk to the egg/sugar mixture and whisk to combine. Pour the mixture back into the saucepan and heat over medium-low heat, cooking 8 to 10 minutes, until it just starts to becomes thick, like heavy cream. The moment the mixture starts to thicken, remove it from heat and continue to whisk for several minutes.

Pour the Cream into four shallow soup bowls and serve warm with a sprinkle of cinnamon on top.

Pasta Lenticchie
Macaroni and Lentils

Serves four

THIS IS A CLASSIC LENTIL DISH with pasta, a kind of poor man's minestrone—flavorful and meaty tasting. Mom never used meat, though. I tried making it with chopped bacon once, but it was all wrong. It disguised the earthy taste of the legumes. Serve it in soup bowls by itself or next to Arroz con Pollo for a true Italia-Rican meal.

1 bag of brown lentils (12 ounces)
2 quarts water
1 bay leaf
1 clove of garlic
2 teaspoons salt
¾ cup olive oil
1 medium carrot, pealed and diced
1 stalk celery, diced fine
1 medium yellow onion, minced fine
2 cups chicken broth (in Basilicata and
    Long Island we just used water!!!)
1 cup tubetini pasta (some folks
    call it macaroni-salad pasta or tubetti)

RINSE THE LENTILS and sift through them with your fingers looking for stray pebbles to remove. Cook the lentils in the water along with 1 teaspoon of the salt, the garlic clove, and the bay leaf. Bring to a boil, then turn down the heat and simmer 20 minutes until the lentils are tender. Discard the bay leaf. Drain the water and reserve both water and lentils separately.

Heat the oil in a skillet and sauté the carrot, celery, and onion until translucent and aromatic. Add the remaining 1 teaspoon salt to taste, and 2 to 3 ladles full of the cooked lentils.

Cook over low heat and mash some of the lentils into a paste with a large wooden spoon.

Add this mixture back into the lentil pot along with enough of the reserved water (or the chicken broth) to make a soupy mixture.

Add the pasta and cook 8 to 10 minutes until pasta is done. (The soup can be thinned with some of the reserved water to your liking.)

Serve immediately. Or when cool, place in the fridge covered overnight and reheat the next day.

Arroz con Pollo
Spanish Fried Rice with Chicken

Serves 4

TAKE A HALF CHICKEN that's already been cooked (or you can start with a fresh chicken, I suppose, but in our house many a meal started with something left over from the night before). Pull the meat off the bone and chop it into one-inch cubes, then place the pieces on a broiler pan and broil them 3 to 4 minutes until the skin is crisp. Set aside and keep warm.

For the Spanish rice, use 3 to 4 cups of cold leftover rice.

Make a mixture just like the one Mom used to start the lentils (1 stalk celery, diced; 1 carrot, diced; and ½ onion, diced and all of them sautéed in a little olive oil). Add a tablespoon of tomato paste or catsup and 2 or 3 tablespoons water stirred in to dilute it. Mix over low heat until well combined, then turn up the heat and add another tablespoon of olive oil, pour the rice into the mixture, and heat the rice for 4 to 5 minutes, just so it becomes coated, and a bit crispy.

Place the rice on individual plates and top with the crispy, warmed chicken.

Verdura
Green Vegetables

Serves 4 as a side dish

4 to 6 cloves garlic, minced
2 Tablespoons fruity olive oil
¼ cup lemon juice
1 Tablespoon balsamic vinegar (back then
  we didn't know nothing from balsamic
  vinegar, so for authenticity use red wine
  vinegar.)
Salt and pepper to taste
¼ to ½ cup water or broth (vegetable or chicken
  stock)
2 bunches (6 to 8 cups) broccolini, cut in 1-inch
  pieces

MINCE AND MASH THE GARLIC into a paste. (If you don't have a can of tomatoes on hand for mashing, you can use the side of a knife.) Place the garlic in a cup along with the oil, lemon juice, vinegar, salt, and pepper. Set aside.

In a small casserole pan, add the water or broth and the broccolini. Cover the pan, and simmer for 8 to 10 minutes, poaching the broccolini to desired doneness.

Remove the broccolini to a serving bowl. Pour the sauce over the top, toss briefly and serve immediately.

Aqua Cotto – Cooked Water

Serves four

JUST LIKE THE WORD "ALOOF" fits with Dad's personality, the title of this recipe fits with Mom's style of cooking (it's such a peasant dish that it's titled "Water"). Besides, the way it looks—and tastes—really jibes with the crazy way our lives went just before we escaped from Queens. There's another dish called aqua pazzo, Crazy Water, that would have worked, too. But that's another story.

> ¼ cup olive oil
> 2 medium onions, thinly sliced
> 4 cups sliced mushroom stems and diced zucchini
> 1 carrot, diced
> 2 cups beet greens, roughly chopped
> Salt and pepper to taste
> 4 cups water (or reduced vegetable stock)
> 1 28-ounce can whole (peeled) tomatoes,
>   broken up, or 4 medium tomatoes, scalded,
>   skinned, and seeded
> ½ loaf stale Italian bread, torn into 1-inch chunks
>   for serving
> grated Parmesan cheese for garnish

IN A CAST IRON STOCK POT, heat the oil to very hot and add the onions, mushroom stems, zuchinni, and carrots. Sauté the mixture over high heat, stirring constantly, until the vegetables are deep brown.

Add the greens and sauté just a few minutes. Add the tomatoes and stock and simmer the soup 10 to 15 minutes over low heat.

Place the bread chunks into soup bowls and ladle the soup on top. Sprinkle some grated Parmesan cheese on top at the table. Be careful! It's hot!

Meatballs

Serves four

THESE ARE THE BEST. They're great with spaghetti and Italian-style tomato gravy. But they're also great alone if you make 'em wet, wet, wet. Dad liked 'em without gravy or broth, on a plate all by themselves (with grated Parmesan cheese on top). Or you can try them in a bowl, on some mashed potatoes, floating in a nice helping of chicken broth.

>1 pound ground beef
>1 cup grated Parmesan cheese
>¼ cup chopped parsley
>2 eggs, beaten
>½ cup minced onion
>4 cloves garlic, minced
>1 cup ricotta cheese
>1/3 to ½ cup breadcrumbs (optional)
>1/3 cup vegetable or light oil for frying

PUT EVERYTHING EXCEPT the breadcrumbs and frying oil into a large bowl and then gush it all together with both hands. Pour in and combine enough of the breadcrumbs to make the meat mixture come together, but not so much that it becomes dry and falls apart.

For each meatball, take a small scoop of meat mixture about the size of a small tangerine and mold it in both hands into a very moist round shape. Set each in turn on a platter when you're done and continue until all the meat is used up. You'll have about 12 to 14 meatballs. Since each meatball will be so moist, feel free to roll each in a separate platter of breadcrumbs, just enough to hold their shape before frying.

In a deep skillet, heat the oil over medium-high heat. When it starts to bubble, and when a little splash of water flicked in with your fingers spits back at you, place about 4 to 6 of the meatballs delicately into the oil. Cook on all sides over medium-high heat 5 or 6 minutes until golden brown. Take one out of the pan at first, and let it cool, then open it up to see if it's done inside. Also, they're not great if the outside isn't crispy, so be sure to use hot, hot oil and try to cook them as quickly as possible.

As usual, when they come out of the oil, drain them on torn-open paper bags or paper towels.

SERVING NOTE: Years later Laura told me she made this recipe as mini meatballs, about as big as small walnuts, and would serve them in a bowl with chicken stock and Parmesan on top. Oooo Mommy!

Zeppole (Mom used to pronounce them "Ezzepole") Sweet Fried Fritters

Yield: 32

WHEN I FIRST WROTE this (ten years ago) there were no recipes available. Now you can find them all over the internet. This is Mom's sweet version. I've tasted some with zucchini and others with bacalao, or salt cod. If anyone has any tips for adjustments, please let me know. It might give me a little more insight into my mom's style of cooking and my upbringing.

1 package dried yeast (1/2 teaspoon)
4 Tablespoons sugar
1 cup milk
2 eggs, beaten
2 Tablespoons vegetable oil
5 cups all-purpose flour
3/4 teaspoon fine sea salt
5 cups of vegetable oil for frying
2/3 cup honey
½ cup of decorettes (or "sprinkles": Laura and I
      used to call them colored ants, and it drove
      Mom nuts), or
½ cup powdered sugar

IN A LARGE BOWL, combine the yeast and the sugar and mix with a wooden spoon. Add the milk, beaten egg, and vegetable oil.

Slowly add the flour while stirring slowly. When all but 1 cup of the flour is added, the mixture will still be moist, but almost ready to come together as a dough. Slowly mix in the remaining flour until it starts to form a medium dough. Knead the dough 5 to 8 minutes.

Let the dough rise for an hour, until it doubles in size.

In a deep casserole, heat the oil. Drop a tablespoon-full of the dough into the hot, bubbling oil one at a time. (Note: Before cooking several at a time, do a test with one of the zeppole to check for proper cooking time. Let the zeppole cool a few minutes, then tear it open to check for doneness and crispiness.) You should be able to get five or six zeppole in the casserole in one batch. Flip them over gently after a few minutes with a couple of wooden spoons to get all sides golden. Reduce heat and fry them 4 to 5 minutes.

Remove the little zeppole to torn-open brown paper bags (a peasant convience) to drain. But paper towels will also do the trick. Repeat with the rest of the zeppole. While they're still warm, drizzle with the honey and then sprinkle with the decorettes.

Or you can "fagetabout" the honey and "colored ants" and just sprinkle them with a light coating of powdered sugar.

Mexican Tacos Italian Style

THIS IS THE MASTERPIECE my Uncle Johnny invented when he opened his restaurant in Hollywood. The dish, I'd say, should be considered Puertorriqueño, but because he knew the gang from Queens was looking for him, Johnny didn't want to have anything to do with being Puerto Rican at that time.

> 2 cooked chicken breasts, shredded
> 2 cups marinara sauce (your favorite, or
>   simply some tomato sauce jazzed up with
>   1/3 cup diced onion, 3 Tablespoons minced
>   green peppers and a small, minced
>   jalapeño, sautéed a few minutes in
>   1 Tablespoon of vegetable oil)
> 6 corn tortillas
> 1 cup vegetable oil, for frying
> 4 cups thinly sliced lettuce (or a combo of lettuce
>   and julienned cabbage)
> 2 medium tomatoes, diced
> 1 cup Queso Fresco, crumbled (feta or
>   cheddar cheese as a substitute)

IN A SMALL SKILLET over medium heat, heat a few tablespoons of the vegetable oil and sauté the onion, green pepper, jalapeño mixture (if you're jazzing up a simple tomato sauce). Heat the sauce until the added ingredients are well incorporated and add the shredded chicken. Sauté a few minutes, then set aside.

Heat the oil in a deep saucepan. Fry the tortillas one at a time in the hot oil until crisp and golden but still pliable, 2 to 3 minutes. (Alternatively, you can heat the tortillas over the flame of the stovetop and flip them over a couple of times.) Fold each of the tortillas over, and stuff each with two to three tablespoons of the chicken/tomato mixture.

Fill each taco with the shredded lettuce, diced tomatoes, then crumble the cheese on top.

Serve with hot sauce or as is.

Orange Salad

Serves 4

MOM NEVER MADE THIS IN NEW YORK, but she must have known about it because she said she learned it from a Jewish lady who went to Miami for the winter.

Something tells me it has a Basilicata twist to it.

Mom peeled a few oranges, broke them up into wedges and put them in a bowl. She covered the oranges with a little olive oil and water, then sprinkled them with salt and pepper. She added her own "California touch," as she called it: a few leaves of fresh mint. Sounds strange, I know, although you haven't heard the weird part. (But have faith; it tastes delicious.) Dad just stuck up his nose and told her that oil and water don't mix. She must have known what he meant because she didn't say a word.

The weird part? The addition of garlic.

4 oranges, peeled and divided into wedges
1 to 2 Tablespoons garlic, minced very, very fine
2 Tablespoons very fruity olive oil
½ teaspoon fine sea salt
½ cup cold water
6 to 8 fresh mint leaves, chopped

PUT EVERYTHING in a small bowl. Toss so the oranges are well coated. Correct for salt. Serve at room temperature or chill in the fridge for a few hours.

Anisette Rusks

As other immigrant ethnicities often did, peasant Italians were habitually coming up with recipes to make use of left-over ingredients. These bread rusks were made with day-old Italian bread and Anisette, an anise-flavored liqueur, which is also great for sipping. Crispy and sweet, these rusks can be eaten alone as an appetizer with a glass of wine. Or you can try them for dessert as a base for a scoop of ice cream, or as a foil for a slice of prosciutto and a wedge of cantaloupe.

Preheat the oven to 225 degrees
1 loaf day-old francese bread (or a one-pound
    French or Italian baguette)
12 ounces Anisette liqueur (eight 1 1/2-ounce
    shot glasses full)

Slice the francese loaf into 16 slices, each ¾ inch thick, on an angle so you end up with 16 oval shapes measuring roughly 6" by 2". If the bread is fresh, place the slices on two 12" by 18" baking trays and place in a toaster oven at 225 degrees for 10 to 15 minutes, until they are dried out a bit.

Using the same two baking trays, pour 4 shots (1 ½-ounce jiggers) of Anisette liqueur in each tray. Place the slices 8 to a tray, and press them into the Anisette, then flip the pieces over and repeat. Do this flipping and pressing maneuver several times in order to soak the bread as best as possible into all of the liqueur.

Bake the rusks for 1 hour 15 minutes, turning the slices over two or three times during baking. Remove them when just crisp, and if some are still soft, place those back in the oven for another 5 or 10 minutes. Allow to cool before serving. They can be stored for up to two weeks in an airtight plastic container.

Lupine Styled Fava Beans

WHEN ITALIAN PEASANT farm families migrated to the New World, they brought their habit of preserving fruits, vegetables, and legumes along with them on the journey. If you grew tomatoes and green beans and couldn't eat them quickly enough, you would make sauce or pickled vegetables for the pantry.

This Lupine recipe uses fava beans instead of Lupine beans because it's what they had on hand.

> 1 ½ pounds fava beans in their pods
>   (1 ½ cup raw beans after removing from
>   pods)
> 1 medium garlic clove, peeled and smashed
>   with the side of a knife
> 1 cup distilled water
> 1 teaspoon salt
> ½ cup dill pickle juice
> ¼ cup white wine vinegar

SHELL THE FAVAS from their pods, leaving the tough outer skin intact. Place the garlic, water, salt, pickle juice, and vinegar in a small saucepan and heat until it boils. Allow to cool 15 minutes. Place the beans in two separate 1 ¾-cup Mason jars and pour half of the brine solution over each. Cover jars with lids and let sit at room temperature a few hours, until cool.

Place the jars in the refrigerator for 2 days, then taste for desired flavor and texture (salty, tangy, and soft to the bite). To eat, bite off the end of each bean and squeeze the inner part into your mouth.

Enjoy.

Cavolfiori Fritti
Fried Cauliflower

JUST AS THE BROWN DERBY will always remind me of my father telling me that if I was going to be a crook, I'd better be a good one, whenever I see a cauliflower I'll always think of this dish and conjure up a picture of my father stopping along the roadside to scavenge free vegetables on his way back home from Lost Wages.

But Mom made use of everything. She never let anything go to waste. Especially the cauliflower. We ate steamed cauliflower; cauliflower casserole with anchovies, pine nuts, raisins, and breadcrumbs; we ate cauliflower with garlic and tomatoes as a sauce for pasta; we ate cavolfiore fritti alla parmigiana, the fried florets I told you about that Mom made the night Dad showed up wearing socks. Try it with some anchovy mayonnaise. Not too healthy, I know, but it'll make you feel good, especially if you've been eating steamed cauliflower all week.

1 head cauliflower, cut into medium florets
3 eggs
1 cup grated Parmesan cheese
2 cups flour
Salt and pepper to taste
3 cups vegetable oil, for frying
A few pinches of coarse sea salt for finishing

BREAK THE CAULIFLOWER into florets and trim their stems so they're not too long. Run the florets under cold water just to rinse off, then pat them dry. Set aside.

Heat the oil in a deep saucepan.

Put the eggs in a shallow dish and beat with a fork. In another shallow bowl put the flour and grated Parmesan cheese and salt and pepper. Mix with your hand to combine.

Place half a dozen or so florets at a time, first in the egg to coat, then in the flour mixture to coat. Then drop them gently into the bubbling oil. Toss as often as necessary so they are all cooked golden brown, then remove to paper towels to drain. Continue with the rest of the cauliflower.

Serve them warm with a few pinches of the sea salt on top, and with anchovy flavored mayonnaise (3 or 4 tablespoons mayonaise, 1 tablespoon anchovy paste, 1/2 lemon, squeezed, and a pinch of pepper) as an appetizer. They're great at room temperature, too.

You could also make a sandwich or a salad out of them.

Mom's Original Parmesan Burgers

Makes 7 to 8 thin burgers (or 3 to 4 thick ones)

BURGERS WERE THE SOUL FOOD for truck drivers, longshoremen, and kids, too, as you could tell by how Manny was inhaling his. These lumps of greasy meat had crunchy edges. When we shaped them, some of the ground beef would squeeze out from under the can to form an irregular border of crunchy bits when they were fried on the hot griddle.

1 pound ground beef
2 eggs, beaten
1 cup grated Parmesan cheese
4 to 6 Tablespoons bread crumbs
6 to 8 Tablespoons minced onions (¼ cup)
Salt and pepper to taste
6 hamburger buns, storebought or homemade
Lettuce, tomato, onion, and pickle and your
favorite garnish dressings

IN A SMALL BOWL, crack and scramble the eggs and set aside.

HERE'S HOW WE MADE 'EM at Ann's Café and you can too.

MOM MIXED A BIG BOWL of ground beef together with some chopped onions, salt, and pepper. Then she threw in a "couple eggs," some grated Parmesan cheese, and a small handful of breadcrumbs. She shaped the ground beef into balls with an ice-cream scoop and placed each one on a piece of wax paper.

Then I took over and covered each ball of ground beef with another sheet of wax paper, and—with a heavy whack—I flattened each one with a large can of Italian pear tomatoes. I don't know if it made a difference if it was tomatoes in the can, but I do know that a number ten can (28 ounces) was the best size (4" diameter) to use for shaping burgers, crushing garlic, and throwing at mice in the storeroom.

After they're all shaped, you can place them on plates and put them in the fridge for an hour or two, until you have to fry them to order on a hot griddle or cast-iron pan about a minute or two per side.

Serve on a toasted bun with your favorite "setup," preferably, lettuce, tomato, onion, and pickle—and a schmear of mayo, catsup, and mustard.

Chili 'n' Beans

THE RAW ONIONS AND CHEDDAR CHEESE added at the end is what makes this recipe extra special.

> 2 to 3 Tablespoons olive oil
> 1 medium onion, diced
> 1 stalk carrot peeled and diced
> 1 stalk celery, diced
> 2 pounds ground beef
> 2 teaspoons salt
> 6 to 8 grinds of black pepper
> 1 28-ounce can whole tomatoes, broken up
>   with their juices
> 1/2 cup red kidney beans, drained
> Diced onions and grated cheddar cheese for garnish

> FOR THE SPICES:
> 1/2 teaspoon each of paprika, cayenne, chili powder,
>   garlic powder, onion powder, and cumin

IN A CASSEROLE, add the olive oil and turn the heat to medium. Add the onion, carrot, and celery and heat 4 to 5 minutes, mixing constantly. Break up the ground beef into the pan, add the salt and sauté 4 to 5 minutes, until partially cooked.

Mix the spice ingredients together in a bowl and set aside.

Add the tomatoes and their juices, and add about half of the spice mixture (about 1 1/2 teaspoons) and simmer another 15 minutes. Add the beans (drained of their juices) 5 minutes before the end of cooking. Correct for salt, pepper, and spices.

Serve with grated cheddar cheese and diced raw onions.

Chili Size

USE ONE OF Mom's Parmesan burgers. Place the toasted bottom bun, the lettuce/tomato/pickle set-up, and cooked patty on top. Then smother it with a healthy scoop of Mom's Chili 'n' Beans. Of course, then sprinkle on the grated cheddar cheese and raw onions. Also toast the other side of the bun and serve it alongside the Chili Size, because you're sure to want it to help you transfer some of the chili to your mouth.

Chocolate Egg Cream

NOBODY MADE THIS IN CALIFORNIA when we arrived, so we were lucky to get it whenever there was a bottle of seltzer (carbonated water) around (not often). So, as an alternative to a soda-fountain spray of carbonated water, one can use one's favorite bottled soda water, perhaps Perrier, San Pellegrino, or your favorite local brand. Sure, it won't be as fizzy, but it will give you a reasonable version.

> Chilled carbonated water from a soda siphon
>   (or your favorite bottled soda water)
> Evaporated milk, or heavy cream
> Hershey's chocolate syrup, or your favorite
>   brand, like Bosco or Trader Joe's Midnight
>   Moo

IF POSSIBLE, use a Coca-Cola style (bell-shaped) glass, because that's what they used in the soda fountain shops in Queens. In the bottom of the glass, put 2 tablespoons of the chocolate syrup. Then add about ¼ cup of the evaporated milk or heavy cream.

Then gently spray the carbonated water (cold) in the glass, while stirring with a long spoon. Serve immediately.

Crumb Cake

UNTIL RECENTLY, I NEVER TASTED A GOOD CRUMB CAKE AGAIN. And I never found a recipe. Years later one of the bakers at Gayle's, Teal Basile, came up with this one. And when I tasted it, I let out a moan, because it reminded me of that night Mom told me about Dad, and how the California crumb cake could never live up to those we had from the bakeries in Queens.

Preheat the oven to 320 degrees
Butter a 9" by 13" baking dish
and line the bottom with parchment paper

Batter ingredients:

7 ounces unsalted butter, soft
1 cup sugar
¼ cup brown sugar
2 eggs
1 cup sour cream
2 ounces milk
2 teaspoons vanilla extract
2 ½ teaspoons baking powder
1 teaspoon kosher salt
2 cups all-purpose flour

Topping Ingredients:

2 cups brown sugar
1 cup sugar
1 ½ teaspoons cinnamon
½ teaspoon kosher salt
1 pound unsalted butter, melted
5 cups all-purpose flour

Batter instructions:

CREAM THE BUTTER and sugar with a wooden spoon or hand-held mixer until light and fluffy. In a separate bowl, whisk together the eggs, sour cream, milk, and vanilla. Add to the butter mixture. In another separate bowl, whisk together the baking powder, kosher salt, and flour. Add it to the butter mixture. Mix until well combined. Place the mixture in a well-greased 9" by 13" baking dish and set aside.

Topping Instructions:

WHISK TOGETHER the brown sugar, sugar, cinnamon, and kosher salt. Pour in the melted butter and stir to combine. Mix in the flour just until it disappears. Set aside until ready to use.

To assemble:

AFTER YOU'VE LEVELED THE BATTER in the baking dish, add the topping evenly.

Bake at 320 degrees for 1 hour, rotating the pan halfway through. Take out of the oven and loosely cover with foil. Bake another 20 minutes until a knife comes out clean.

Lemon Meringue Pie

THIS RECIPE MAY BE similar to the one I used as a teenager.

Louisa Beers, our partner at Gayle's and a fine creative baker herself, found this recipe in her mother Goldie's vintage, hand-written recipe book. It looks to me like a simple, 1950s-style recipe.

The recipe is best done in a 9" Pyrex-style glass pie plate.

Preheat oven to 350 degrees

For the crust:

> 12 graham crackers, crushed, or 1 1/2 cups graham
>   cracker crumbs
> 1/3 cup sugar
> 1/4 to 1/3 cup melted butter

IN A BOWL CONTAINING THE CRUMBS AND SUGAR, slowly add the butter while mixing to combine. Add only enough butter so that the mixture comes together when squeezed with your hand. Press firmly into the bottom and sides of the glass pie plate with your hands or the bottom of a round measuring cup.

Prebake the crust for about 10 minutes and let cool before filling.

For the filling:

> 3 large egg yolks
> 1 can Eagle Brand sweetened condensed milk
> 1/2 cup lemon juice

In a bowl, whisk the egg yolks, then whisk in the condensed milk, then the lemon juice. Pour the filling mixture into the prebaked crust.

Bake for 8 to 9 minutes, until you can see that the filling has firmed up when wiggled. Allow the pie to cool for 5 to 10 minutes.

For the meringue:

> 3 to 4 egg whites, at room temperature
> a few pinches of salt
> 1/4 teaspoon cream of tartar (optional)
> 1/3 cup of sugar

PLACE THE EGG WHITES IN A STAINLESS STEEL BOWL over a very low heat on your stove top. Whisk a few minutes until just warm to the touch. Remove from the heat and whisk in the salt and the cream of tartar (if you're using it).

Using a hand mixer or stand mixer, on medium speed, slowly add the sugar. Increase the speed to high. After 6 to 8 minutes of vigorous mixing, the whites should form stiff peaks. Spread the mixture over the top of the pie, taking care to seal the meringue to the edge of the crust.

Bake for about 8 minutes, until the swirl tips of the meringue are just colored.

Minestrone

SINCE I'VE BEEN IN THE FOOD BUSINESS for more than 65 years, I've run across many variations of numerous dishes. This one is a combination of what my mother made and one Gayle and I had at a restaurant in Montepulciano, Italy. In that wonderful version, the cooks took a portion of the cooked vegetables, passed it through a food ricer, and added it back into the soup to create a thick and unctuous consistency. In my version, I use an immersion blender.

4 Tablespoons olive oil
1 medium carrot, diced
1 medium stalk celery, diced
2 small (or one large) yellow onion, diced
1 teaspoon kosher salt
5 grinds black pepper
4 medium size cloves garlic, minced
2 small zucchini, cut into large, diced pieces
4 to 5 cups water
1 teaspoon Better than Bullion stock flavoring (optional)
1 left over Parmesan cheese rind, about 3" to 4"
1 bay leaf
½ pound green beans, trimmed and sliced into 1 ½ inch
       pieces (about 3 cups)
5 medium pear tomatoes
1 15 ½ ounce can Cannellini beans
1 or 2 teaspoons of your favorite Italian herbs (dried or
       fresh thyme, basil, savory)
Parmesan cheese and extra virgin olive oil for serving

* * * *

IN A MEDIUM STOCK POT, add the olive oil, carrots, celery, and onion and set the heat to medium high. Add the salt and pepper and sauté several minutes, while stirring. Set the heat to low and continue while stirring for 6 to 7 minutes. Add the garlic halfway through the cooking time. If the pot dries out, it's okay to add another few tablespoons of olive oil.

When the vegetables are just browned a bit, add the diced zucchini and green beans. Cook the mixture over low heat, stirring constantly for 3 to 4 minutes.

Add 4 cups of the water (reserving one cup to use, if necessary, later). Add the teaspoon of Better than Bullion and the bay leaf. Cook 15 minutes over medium low heat, stirring occasionally.

In a separate pot of boiling water, scald the tomatoes for a minute or two and remove with a slotted spoon to cool. Slice the tomatoes in half, squeeze out the seeds and remove the skins. Dice into 1 inch pieces. Add the tomatoes to the soup and cook another 10 to 15 minutes.

Turn off the heat and, in a small separate casserole, pour in around two cups of the soup mixture. With an immersion blender (or in a ricer, if you have one), puree the mixture completely into a paste. Then add it back to the large pot along with the cannellini beans and herbs and warm a few more minutes.

Correct for salt and pepper.

Serve in soup plates with a drizzle of extra virgin olive oil and a sprinkle of Parmesan cheese.

Acknowledgements:

Friends, Associates, Writers Support Group:

Gayle Ortiz, for life inspiration, business acumen, and much love and support through 55 years of marriage.

Louisa Beers, for being the ideal business partner, a fine cook and baker in her own right, and a recipe "taster" par-excellence, and the one who provided her mother Goldie's Lemon Meringue pie recipe.

Kathryn Chetkovich, for years of theater libretti (most notably *Smoke*), developmental editing (on this and other projects), and writing inspiration.

Barbara Arroyo, for having been the recipe developer and chief cook at Gayle's Rosticceria for 40 years.

Sarah Rabkin, for editing comments and advice over the course of many projects, not to mention having reviewed at least five drafts of this memoir.

Steve McGuirk, a long-time friend and the father of our god children, Laurel, Colin, and Evan, for editing advice on many of these pages as well as other fiction and non-fiction projects,

Roger Bunch, for editing advice on many of these pages as well as other fiction and non-fiction projects, and especially for reading one of the first advance reader editions of the book.

Steve "Spike" Wong, for writing inspiration and theater guidance on many projects.

Mark Marinovich, for support in agent searches and numerous edits of letters and Capitola Soquel Times installments.

Michael Scott, for numerous therapy sessions in which we explored many of the stories from the book and the numerous intricacies of my mental process in writing it.

Catherine Segurson, editor and founder of *Catamaran Literary Reader,* for publishing several of my early stories that are an important part of this memoir.

Theater Associates:

Greg Fritsch, my long-time friend and theater associate (as co-librettist, director, and music arranger) in all five of my theater pieces: *Smoke Cabaret, Bread - The Musical, Circus, Kitchen Kabaret,* and *Over the Roof* (formerly *Escaping Queens*).

Jon Nordgren, for having had the wisdom and trust to accept and produce *Escaping Queens* at Cabrillo Stage for two sold-out seasons in 2012 and 2013.

Lori Rivera, long-time theater associate and the singer/ actress who has performed in every one of my productions.

Adam Saucedo, actor and singer par-excellence, who has appeared in many of my shows.

Matt Shelton, former owner of Shelton Theater in San Francisco, who produced sucessful runs (through several seasons) of *Smoke, Bread,* and one of the most successful concert readings of *Escaping Queens* we've ever presented.

Max Bennett-Parker, quadruple threat as actor, singer, accompanist, and arranger in several of my productions.

Wyatt Bernard, for playing the role of Little Joey in the original produciton of *Escaping Queens,* and whose image adorns the cover of *Pastina.*

Jana Marcus, for outstanding publicist work on the *Escaping Queens* run at Cabrillo Stage and for designing the cover of this book.

Tucker Gold, for his exceptional rendition of "Cowboy" in *Escaping Queens* at Shelton Theater in 2017.

Foodies and Recipe Testers:

Marcie Bei, for food inspiration and for testing several recipes toward the end of the book's editing stage.

John Bei, former chef at the restaurant at DeLaveaga Golf Course, who has been a valued customer and confidant at Gayle's for many years.

Gunnar Amundson, for recipe testing and many great "meetings" under the influence of his stellar homemade beer.

Mary and Ernie Tavella, for recipe testing and inspirational support as great neighbors.

Teal Basile, long time pastry recipe developer at Gayle's and a great tester for several recipes.

Barbara Arroyo, for having been the recipe developer and chief cook at Gayle's Rosticceria for 40 years.

Sarah Rabkin, for testing Meatballs, Chocolate Egg Cream, and Orange Salad.

From *Over The Roof* (formerly *Escaping Queens*):

Origins of the song "Cowboy"

I'VE ALREADY MENTIONED that the musical, *Over the Roof* (formerly titled *Escaping Queens*) is drawn from this memoir. What I haven't mentioned is that the abuse scene (which appears in Chapter Sixteen) in the memoir and in the musical (which serves as the climax) are identical, having only been revealed to me through the writing of both projects and 60 years of self-therapy. The fact that they both happen at Ann's Café in Wilmington, California is testimony to the fact that, despite my many years of repressing the memory—and the final breakthrough of remembering the event—it was one of the great rewards of my being willing to look deeper into my father's chaotic lifestyle. And in the end, I sense it to be a valid form of self-realization.

It helped that my co-author of the musical, Greg Fritsch, prodded me in the final ten years of the show's development, to write a final song for little Joey in which he painfully, and perhaps innocently, conveys what any child might say in fantasy to an abusive father what he may never have had the courage to say to him in person.

MY ORIGINAL EXPERIENCE of using fantasy to escape my parents' wild and crazy relationship was to imagine voluptuous cowgirls fashioned after Marilyn Monroe and Rita Hayworth riding on "stallions" across the bedroom walls to fall asleep.

That image, possibly being too farfetched and risqué, and not quite fitting into the new *Over the Roof* storyline, Greg and I decided to morph the image into one of "Cowboys." Cowboys seemed appropriate for our story arc at that moment in the musical because Little Joey was obsessed with Western movies, gun-toting heroes, and side-kick characters in his anticipation of the family escaping to the freedom and adventure of Southern California—and Hollywood.

Both Greg and our then-musical-director, Max Bennett-Parker always said it was perhaps my best composition. And I tend to agree. The song turns out to be the climax of child abuse that convinces Mama, once and for all, to kick her husband Herman out of the house for good.

"Cowboy"

Gonna ride on outta town
Sleep out under the stars
There won't be no more fences
Keepin' me from goin'

Listen to coyotes
Howlin' in the wind
Won't be no more bad guys
Trailin' after me

Oooooo, COWBOY
What you gonna do
Now that I'm standin' up to you?
Have some respect, mister
Spit that cig'rette out ya mouth
This time you'll be the one who's gettin' burned . . .
Not me

Don't put your hand down by your gun
I'll take a stand, not gonna run (this time)
. . . COWBOY

Don't put ya dukes up in my face
I'll drag your hide all over this place (this time)
. . . COWBOY

If you lift your hand to me
You'll be surprised what you might see
Take your best shot . . . . COWBOY

You know I will stand up to you
You won't believe what I can do (this time) . . .

(spoken) What's wrong?

Cowboys don't cry
Cowboys get along
That's only dust in your eye . . . Cowboy . . . Don't cry

Gonna break outta this corral
It's so peaceful out on the range
Just me and the doggies and the moon

Now I gotta go
Kick that ol' campfire out
Get up on my horse and ride away . . .
COWBOY . . . Ride away

∾ *Pastina*